AF632965

KAIVALYADHAMA

Where Yoga tradition and Science meet

KAIVALYADHAMA

Where Yoga tradition and Science meet

POPULAR YOGA

PRĀṆĀYĀMA

SWAMI KUVALAYANANDA

KAIVALYADHĀMA,
Swami Kuvalayananda Marg,
Lonavla (410103), INDIA

First Published : January, 1931
Fifth Edition : January, 1972
Sixth Edition : 1977
Seventh Edition : 1983
Eighth Edition : 1999
Ninth Edition : 2000
Tenth Edition : April, 2005
Eleventh Edition : April, 2010
Twelfth Edition : January, 2016
Thirteenth Edition : December, 2020
Reprints : April, 2022
Reprints : June, 2024
Printed in India

ISBN : 81 - 902803-6-8

Price : ₹ 300/-

Published by
Shri O. P. Tiwari, Secretary,
Kaivalyadhama, S. M. Y. M. Samiti,
Swami Kuvalayananda Marg,
Lonavla - 410 403

Printed at
Ace Enterprises,
Madhu-Raj Nagar,
137/A Paud Road,
Pune - 410 038.

PREFACE

मूकं करोति वाचालं पङ्गुं लङ्घयते गिरिम् ।
यत्कृपा तमहं वन्दे परमानन्दमाधवम् ।।

(Reverence to Mādhava, the Supreme Bliss !
Blessed by Him the dumb shall grow eloquent
and the lame shall stride across a Mountain)

It is after fifteen years that we are presenting to the public our handbook of Prāṇāyāma. No doubt, in the meanwhile we published Prāṇāyāma Part Two, in 1958. But the Prāṇāyāma Part Two although containing six varieties of Prāṇyāma that had not been included in Part One and also giving very valuable articles on the subject of Prāṇāyāma, could not present the subject of Prāṇāyāma in its proper perspective. Thus the public remained starved of Prāṇāyāmic food for a very long time. During all these years the demand for a tolerably complete handbook on this subject continued.

Now we have great pleasure in presenting this very comprehensive handbook on the subject of Prāṇāyāma and we are sure it will receive the same appreciation and patronage from the public that our publications have been receiving for the last four decades. In the present handbook we have included all the eight varieties of Prāṇāyāma that are advocated by the authors of Haṭha-Yoga, with a somewhat cursory reference to the four varieties of that subject as taught by Patañjali. The lengthy article on 'Respiration' and also an article on the 'Physiological and Spiritual Values of Prāṇāyāma' which form an important part of the subject as they provided an essential background for clearly understanding it, but which did not appear in Part, have been retained. Thus we have tried our best to make the present handbook of Prāṇāyāma as comprehensive as possible. We must, however, make it clear to our readers that though this handbook is complete in itself, it is no substitute for our quarterly journal *Yoga-Mīmāṃsā,* because that journal contains vast scientific information in the form of actual Laboratory experiments and also many articles on Prāṇāyāma. This information could not be included in this handbook because of its limited scope and also because of the type of readers for whom it is intended. Some of the articles which had appeared in Prāṇāyāma Part Two and which were borrowed from *Yoga-Mīmāṃsā* have also been omitted here. These omissions, however, will not come in the way of our readers' understanding the subject in its basic form.

The great importance of the practice of Prāṇāyāma is clearly brought out in the last Chapter of this handbook but the treatment of the subject is from the modern point of view. Hence it was thought desirable to note here something that our ancient authors have said about Prāṇāyāmic values, both physiological and spiritual.

Manu, one of the greatest ancient law-givers, observes that Prāṇāyāma is a specific remedy against the evil tendency of the mind and the sense organs.[1-2] Kulluka commenting on these observations explains the evil tendencies of the mind as 'Love and Hatred'; and the evil tendencies of the sense organs as the attractions of these organs towards the external objects.[3] These natural tendencies of the mind and the sense organs are condemned as evil because success in Yoga depends upon the introversion of the mind and the sense organs. A similar view is expressed by the

---

1. इंद्रियाणा दह्यन्ते दोषाः प्राणस्य निग्रहात् । M.S. VI 71
2. प्राणायामैर्दहेद्दोषान् । M.S. VI 72
3. मनसो रागादयाश्चक्षुरादेश्च विषयप्रवणत्वादयः । Kullūka

author of Haṭha Pradīpikā[4] saying that some Yoga experts were of the same opinion, that is they considered Prāṇāyāmic alone would be sufficient to overcome the evil tendencies of the mind and sense organs.

Patañjali, the greatest exonent of Yoga Śāstra gives in his two Sūtras,[5] namely II. 52 and 53, a clear exposition of the spiritual values of Prāṇāyāma. The spiritual development of a student of Yoga depends upon two things. First, he must eliminate the factor that obscures the spiritual light and secondly, he must be able to fix his wandering mind. According to Patañjali a student of Yoga is able to make a beginning in both these directions by practising Prāṇāyāma.

Thus far we have taken notice of the importance of Prāṇāyāma from the point of view of the ancient authors of the subject of Yoga. We had to touch this point here as it was not discussed either in Part One or Part Two of Prāṇāyāma. previously published.

Now we shall indicate some additional features about the present handbook.

As usual we have very rightly illustrated the subject that is under discussion in this handbook. Every effort is made the handbook thoroughly instructive as well as interesting.

Cautions have been pronounced at every step, making the text-book a reliable and safe guide for a practical student of Prāṇāyāma. Inspite of this fact we would strongly advise everyone first to get himself trained under an expert, if possible, and then take up this handbook for guidance.

---

4. प्राणायामेनैव सर्वे प्रशुष्यन्ति मला इति । H.P.II 37.

5. ततः क्षीयते प्रकाशावरणम् । Pāt. Y. S. II 52.
   धारणासु च योग्यता मनसः । Pāt. Y. S. II 53.

Three important appendices have been attached to this handbook. The general hints contained therein have been based upon our clinical experience at the Āśrama. The insertion of these appendices in this handbook, is intended to make it throughly useful to the practical student of Yoga.

The glossary very tersely gives anatomical and physiological information which has been detailed in *Yoga-Mīṃāṃsā. It will, however,* serve as a valuable guide to a practical student of Yoga and will make him independent of any text-book of anatomy and physiology.

From what has been said upto now in this Preface, this handbook can be called to be the fourth impression of Prāṇāyāma because the largest part of it is taken from Part One although it contains some chapters borrowed from Part Two.

The present handbook of Prāṇāyāma owes its publication to Messrs Popular Prakashan of Bombay. They have spared no pains to make it as attractive, instructive and helpful as possible. This firm of publishers has already put in the market our handbook of Āsanas. Our best thanks are due to them for having undertaken to publish our writings simply for the love of our ancient culture interpreted in the light of modern science and thought.

We have no words to express adequately our gratitude to our readers. They have taken very sympathetically to whatever we have written on the science and practice of Yoga inspite of many a shortcomings for which these writings suffer.

We cannot close this short Preface without mentioning a word about our service to Yoga. Our personal share in this service is very small. The overwhelmingly largest share belongs to our Āśramite Brothers. They are highly qualified university men most disinterestedly devoted to the cause of Yoga. Even those brothers who have no university qualification are men of sublime culture and have given decades of their precious life to the cause of Yoga. May God bless them all !

May the cause of Yoga prosper and may it bring peace to the war-weary world !

KUVALAYANANDA

Kaivalyadhama,
Lonavala, (C.Rly.)
15th March, 1966

PREFACE

Kaivalyadhama is happy to present the 11th edition of **PRĀṆĀYĀMA** to the readers and lovers of Yoga. As you know Swami Kuvalayananda was the first person to initiate and promote the scientific investigation into the traditional aspect of Yoga. Based on scientific findings he had critically edited widely acclaimed books of Asana and Prāṇāyāma. The work we initiated will always be remembered in the World of Yoga. He was not a person seeking fame as he always said

माना पमानो यावेतौ योगिनस्तो विषामृतम् ।
अपमानोऽमृतं प्राहुर्मानस्तु विषम् विषम् ।।

Meaning that an honour to a Yogi is poison while disrespect helps him to grow and act as an ambrosia. The book Prāṇāyāma is still regarded as the best, though he left us in the year 1966. We could not improve upon his work. Needless to say, it contains most systematic, scientific and techniques explained is simple and terse manner. I am sure readers will continue to practice and take advantage of his valuable contribution as he said -

"Yoga has a complete message for humanity. It has a message for the human body. It has a message for the human mind. And it has also a message for the human spirit. Will rich men with their money and young intelligent and healthy men with their selfless service, come forth to help the Kaivalyadhama to take this message, to the farthest corner of the World ?"

- O. P. Tiwari

Preface to the Twelfth Edition

It gives me great pleasure to present to you the twelfth and fully revised edition of *Prāṇāyāma* by Swami Kuvalayanandaji.

This book provides deep insight into the history, philosophy, and techniques for practice of different pranayamas as per the Hatha Yoga Tradition. It presents, with sound scientific evidence, the anatomical and physiological changes and benefits a practitioner experiences during practice. Further, it helps to make the actual practice of pranayama more effective as a practitioner is able to discern between the essential and optional parts of its different techniques. This book, coupled with Swami Kuvalayanandaji's book *Asana* are bibles for those practitioners looking to further their study in the discipline in yoga.

The Kaivalyadhama family has played a major role in the review, editing, and redrafting of this work. I am especially grateful to Swami Maheshanandaji for his thoughtful guidance and advice. Equally, I am thankful to Mrs. Pushpa Mandke, Mr. Ravindranath Bodhe, and Ms. Eela Dubey for their contributions towards giving this book its final shape. Lastly, I would like to recognize our publisher, Mr. Nitin Tanpure, who has continued to be of great support over many years for his publishing services.

In 1924 Swami Kuvalayanandaji wrote "Yogic culture is one of the richest legacies the ancient Indian savants have left to the world. The noble spiritual elevation that is seen in India even in her present deplorable condition is mainly due to the influence of yoga in one form or another. A revival of this culture is sure to raise her to her forme position of glorious dignity."

I hope that the twelfth edition of this book will be welcomed by yoga lovers around the world.

- O. P. Tiwari

Preface to the new Edition

We all know that Swami Kuvalayanandji has won a laurel for India in the sense that he has ushered in a scientific temper in the field of Yoga. His scientific activities are considered to be the pioneering work in the frontiers of Yoga Research. The book *Prāṇāyāma* authored by him is a masterpiece of its kind.

This book gives a comprehensive understanding of the science of pranayama in accordance with the Hatha Yoga-tradition. It also provides a good insight into the history, philosophy and the techniques of *Prāṇāyāma* coupled with the scientific evidence towards the validation of ancient science. The book may be considered as a Bible for the seekers and practitioners of this wonderful science.

The Philosophico-Literary Research Department of Kaivalyadhama Lonavala has taken a great initiative in bringing out the new reprint of this wonderful work in a more attractive form under the guidance of Swami Maheshanandji, Chairman, Kaivalyadhama Ashram, Lonavala, we are grateful to him. We also extend our thankfulness to Prof. Ravindranath Bodhe for his erudite advice.

The thirteenth Edition of '*Prāṇāyām*' comes with a new wave of breadth literally. It is revamped with a new cover design by Mr. Shrish Badekar - Art Teacher of our School Kaivalya Vidhya Niketan. He also had a major role to play in designing and drawing appropriate sketches

Our Yoga Achraya Mrs. Sandhay Dixit laboriously and painstakingly went to the detailed contents of the book sharing her expertise to make the book more meaningful and user friendly. More importantly we have integrated the photos and figures in the contents and narrative of the book itself and have not kept the figures in the last pages of the books as an appendix. I acknowledge the contribution of the printer Mr. Nitin Tanpure towards the smooth and quality publication of the book.

I fervently hope that this new reprint of the precious book will definitely cater to the needs of the readers and Yoga aspirants across the globe.

I pray to the Shri Adinatha, the Primordial Teacher of Hatha Yoga, to shower his blessings on this profound piece of work.

Thank you.

O.P. Tiwari
Secretary, Kaivalyadhama,
Shriman Madhava Yoga Mandir Samiti,
Lonavala.

CONTENTS

LIST OF ILLUSTRATIONS

ABBREVIATIONS

आश्वालायनश्रौतसूत्र	-	आश्व.श्रौ.	-	Āśv. Sr.
घेरंडसंहिता	-	घे. सं	-	Ghe. Smt
जीवन्मुक्तिविवेक	-	जी. मु. वि.	-	Jī. Mu. Vi.
पातञ्जल्योगसूत्र	-	पात. यो. सू.	-	Pāt. Y. S.
बृहद्योगियाज्ञवल्क्यस्मृति	-	बृ. या. स्मृ.	-	Brhadyogi Yā. Sm.
बौधायनधर्मसूत्र	-	बौधा. ध.	-	Baud. Dh.
भगवद्गीता	-	भ. गी	-	B. G.
लघुयोगवासिष्ठ	-	ल. यो. वा.	-	L. Y. V
विद्यारण्य	-	वि. ण्य.	-	V. Ṇya
हठप्रदीपिका	-	हठ. प्र.	-	H. P.

SCHEME OF TRANSLITERATION

अ - a; आ - ā; इ - i; ई - ī; उ - u; ऊ- ū;
ऋ- ṛ; ॠ - ṝ; ऌ - lṛ; ॡ - lṝ; ए - e; ऐ - ai;
ओ - o; औ - au;
अनुस्वार - ṃ; विसर्ग - ḥ;

क् - k; ख् - kh; ग् - g; घ् - gh; ङ् - ṅ;
च् - c; छ् - ch; ज् - j; झ् - jh; ञ् - ñ;
ट् - ṭ; ठ् - ṭh; ड् - ḍ; ढ् - ḍh; ण् - ṇ;
त् - t; थ् - th; द् - d; ध् - dh; न् - n;
प् - p; फ् - ph; ब् - b; भ् - bh; म् - m;
य् - y; र् - r; ल् - l; व् - v;
श् - ś; ष् - ṣ; स् - s;
ह् - h; क्ष् - kṣ; त्र् - tr; ज्ञ् - jñ;

CHAPTER I

RESPIRATION

PRĀṆĀYĀMA is a Yogic exercise in respiration. It is therefore desirable that a student of Prāṇāyāma is acquainted with some important details of the respiratory system. Hence, we propose to describe in this chapter a few broad features of the anatomy and physiology of respiration.

Respiration consists of the alternate expansion and contraction of the thorax, by means of which air is drawn into or expelled from the lungs. In this chapter we shall first consider the various organs that are directly concerned with this passage of air to and from the lungs; and then we shall see how these organs act in the different stages of respiration.

The organs of respiration may be enumerated as the nose, the pharynx, the larynx, the trachea, the bronchi and the lungs. Nerves and blood-vessels connected with these parts may also be looked upon as organs of respiration. Generally, however, the nose is not included in such an enumeration. But when we want to write on respiration from the Yogic point of view, the nose has not only to be included but also to be studied in detail. In dealing with these organs we shall proceed along the passage of the air from outside into the lungs and as we meet with the nose first, we shall start this chapter with a description of that organ.

THE NOSE - - We shall be able to study the nose both externally and internally with the help of a mirror and of the charts given in this chapter. In using this mirror the reader should allow light to come from his back and fall upon the mirror held in his front. The mirror should be so adjusted as would easily throw reflected light into the nostrils when the head is thrown backward, but would not dazzle the eye.

We always see our nose in the mirror. But what we generally see is only the external part of the nostrils. Let our reader have a peep into the internal portions of the nostrils also. He will find that by the side of the dividing wall, up in the cavity there is a hole in each of the two nostrils. He might think that these holes are a sort of communication between the nose and some other organ situated inside the head. But he would be seriously wrong in thinking that way. In fact the external nose is only a small part of the organ anatomically known as the *nose*. The most important part of it is situated inside the head, behind the two holes our reader has seen, and above the hard palate that forms a part of the roof of his mouth. We shall presently examine this internal part of the nose. But before we do so let us finish with the external part of that organ.

If we feel our nose with our fingers, we find that a very large part of it is mobile. This is because this portion of the nose, including the dividing septum, is made of different cartilages attached to one another by a tough. Fibrous membrane and covered over by the skin. If our reader again looks into his mirror and examines the inside of his nostrils, he will find that the skin which covers the external surface of the nose, continues inward and also covers the lower chamber of the internal nose. He will find even the lower portion of the septum clothed similarly in skin. This portion of the nasal cavity is called the *vestibule*. From the walls of this vestibule, our reader will find, a number of stout and stiff hair projecting. Out of these hair, those that grow from the front part project backward, whereas those that rise from the back part project forward. Thus a sievelike arrangement is provided just at the entrance of the nose. The external nose has two ends. The upper end which is connected with the forehead is called the root and the lower end which is free, is called the *apex* of the nose.

If we again feel the flexible part of our nose and examine the upper as well as posterior borders of it, we find them hard. This is because the elastic part of the nose is attached to bones at the top behind. In Fig.2 the mobile nose has been removed and bones to which it is attached are exposed to our view. Our reader will immediately see that the bony borders which carried the flexible attachments of the nose, represent a picture exactly similar to that of the heart drawn in the playing cards. Let us observe a few facts about this bony aperture that directly concern us. Below the forehead and between the eyes there are two bones which we can feel externally. They are called the *nasal bones (1)* and form what is known as the bridge *of the nose.* A vertical line *(3)* is seen dividing the aperture into two exact halves. This represents the nasal septum. The circular curves at the bottom belong to the two upper jaw-bones. *(5)*. These curves mark the lower borders of the two holes observed by our reader in the back part of his external nose.

We have already stated that the external nose is only a small part of the real organ. The most important part of it is situated inside the head. We have now removed the mobile nose and come to the entrance of the inner cavities. Let us now note what is there inside the aperture that lies before us in Fig. 2.

The aperture which is divided into two halves by the nasal septum leads to two cavities that tare roughly speaking ovalshaped.

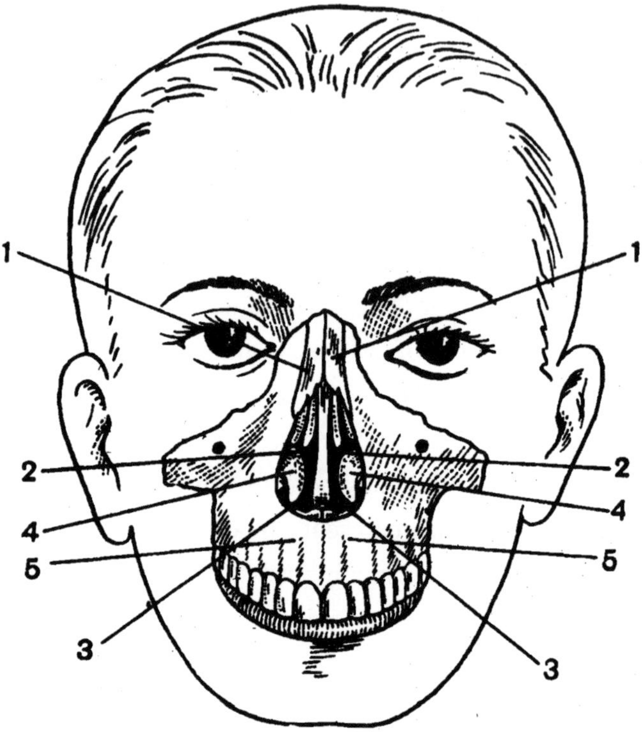

FIG. 2. - Face with the Mobile Nose Cut off and the Nasal Bones and Cavities, with the Upper Jaw-Bones Exposed.

1. The Nasal Bones. 2 The Nasal Cavities. 3 The Nasal Septum. 4 Scroll-like Bones. 5 The jaw-Bones.

These cavities continue backward and open into the throat with holes similar to those we observe on the bony surface before us. Each of these cavities has a floor, a roof, and a medical and a lateral wall.

The septum which divides these cavities stands for the medial wall of both. It is made of bones all along except in front where a large cartilage fills up the gap. The floor is also bony. A reference to Fig. 1 *a* will show this floor in a median section. It is made of two bones. The front part is made of the upper jawbones and the back part, of the hard palate bones. There are two upper jaw-bones and two hard palate bones. The upper jaw-bones are arranged side by side and form our upper jaw in which the teeth are set. Behind

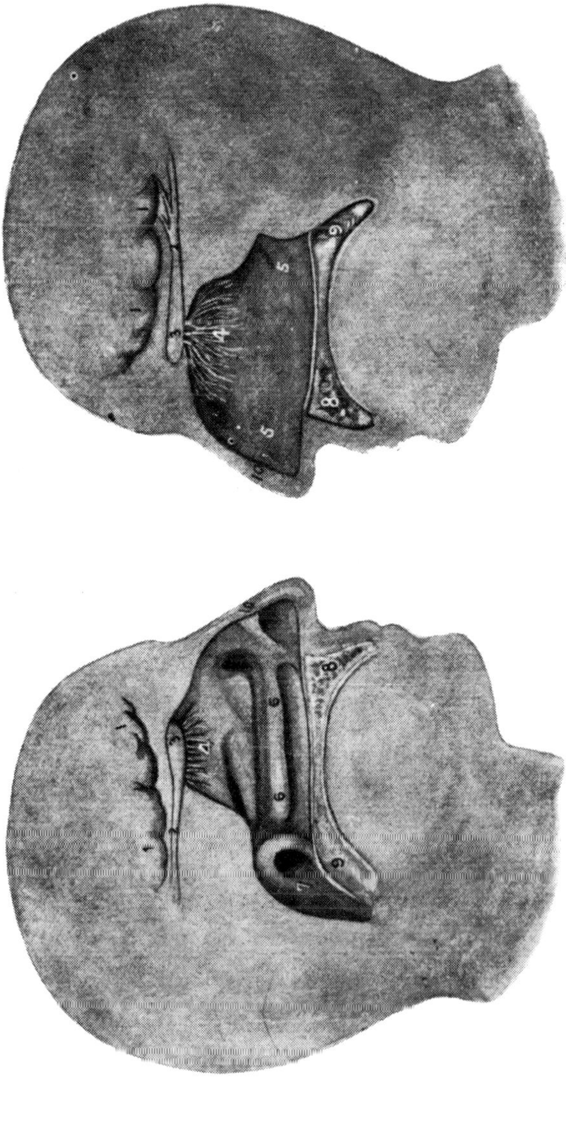

a b

FIG. 1. - Median Section the Head Indicating the Respiratory Tract, etc.
1. Base of the Brain 2. Olfactory Tract 3. Olfactory Bulb 4. Branches of the Olfactory Nerves 5. The Septum of the Nose 6. Bony Folds of the Nose 7. Eustachian Tube 8. The Hard Palate 9. The Soft Palate 10. Mobile Part of the Nose.

the upper jaw, the hard palate bones stand side by side and form our hard palate. The lower surface of the two upper jaw-bones and the hard palate bones go to form the roof of our mouth. If we try to feel the roof of our mouth with our finger from the upper teeth backward, we will meet with two hard surface. One is rough and the other is smooth. The rough surface which we feel just above our teeth is presented by the upper jaw-bones, and the hard but smooth surface that we cross when the finger is moved backward belongs to the hard palate bones. Behind this the soft palate can easily be felt. Fig. 1 shows that the upper surface of the upper jaw-bones and the hard palate bones are horizontal and that is why the floor of the nasal cavities is also horizontal. So the upper jaw-bones and the hard palate bones at once form the roof of the mouth and the floor of the nose. That means the nasal cavities lie just above the roof of the mouth. The lateral walls of the nasal cavities are somewhat complicated. They are also made of bones They rise from below at some distance from the septum, but as they rise they incline towards the septum to meet it at the roof. Some idea of this inclination of the lateral walls can be had from Fig. 2. Here the bony aperture represents the external borders of these nasal walls. So these cavities are broad below, but narrow down at the top. From the lateral walls arise inside the cavities scrolllike bones. One of them has been marked in Fig. 2 *(4).* These scroll-like bones extend all long the length of the lateral walls and open backward into the throat.

Now we consider the roof. This is also a bony structure. The floor of the nasal cavities is horizontal; but the roof is arched. An idea of this arch can be had from Fig. 1 *b,* where the septum is shown arching at the top. Now this septum rises direct to meet the roof, and therefore the upper curve of the septum fairly represents the arch of the roof. We may note especially two bones that form the roof. The nasal bones that have already been noticed form the front slope of the arching roof. Behind these nasal bones the roof is formed by a big bone called *ethmoid*. The ethmoid is at once the roof of the nose and a part of the floor of the brain. That means it separates the nasal cavities from the brain. Thus the nasal cavities stand between the mouth and the brain; and open backwards into the throat just above the soft palate.

Upto now we have studied the bony structure of external nose as well as of the nasal cavities. Now we have to note that these hard surfaces recovered over with mucous membrane. This mucous membrane is a continuous piece that lines out the inside of the external nose except the vestibule, but it also clothes the floor, the roof and the walls of the nasal cavities and continue into the pharynx. When we examine this mucous membrane covering the nasal cavities, we find that functionally two areas are to be mapped out. The upper area covers one third of the total surface of the nasal cavities and the lower area the remaining two-thirds. Having the sense of smell situated in it, the upper district is called the *olfactory region*, the lower district being called the *respiratory region*, as it constitutes the passage for air breathed in and out during respiration. That means the cavities of the nose have got two separate tracts for the two different functions they perform. If we divide the height of the nostrils into three equal parts, the uppermost part is used for smelling and two lower parts are used for breathing. None should suppose, however, that the uppermost part is not at all available as a passage for respiration. Although in the normal and quiet breathing only the lower two parts are used, in forced breathing the upper third is also utilized. The sense of smell, however, is confined to the upper third only, having nothing to do with the two lower regions. This is because the sense of smell depends upon the presence of the olfactory nerve-endings which are distributed only over the upper third area. (Vide Fig. 1(4)).

Two features which distinguish the mucous membrane covering the olfactory region from that covering the respiratory tract, deserve our attention here. The mucous membrane which clothes the respiratory tract is thick and spongy whereas that which lines the olfactory region is softer and more delicate. The other distinguishing feature is the very great vascularity of the respiratory tract. In fact it is marked by the presence of a rich venous plexus. These anatomical facts have a physiological significance. As noted above in ordinary quiet breathing, the air moves through the lower two-thirds of the nasal area. The air in the upper one-third is scarcely disturbed. Now that portion of the mucous membrane which lines the passage of the air must be stouter than the portion where the air is stationary the hours of normal breathing. The greater vascularity of the respiratory tract has also a purpose to serve. When external air is to be breathed into the lungs, it must be warm and moist, otherwise it may have an injurious effect upon the delicate structure of the lungs. Now the large supply of venous blood which is present in the plexus situated in the respiratory region, raises the temperature of the air during inspiration and also moistens it.

It has been stated above that the sense of smell is situated in the upper one-third of the nasal cavities. This sense consists of very fine nerve filaments from twelve to twenty in number. They are distributed like a thick brush both on the septum and the lateral walls. Here these nerves descend through the ethmoid bone which, as we have seen above, separates the nasal cavities from the brain. Through the ethmoid the olfactory nerves reconnected with the olfactory bulb which in its turn is joined to the base of the brain through the olfactory tract. Fig. 1 illustrates the olfactory nerves, the bulb, the tract as also the base of the brain. When the fine endings of the olfactory nerves are stimulated by particles carrying odour with them, sensation of smell is experienced.

Following facts may be remembered with advantage in regard to the sense of smell.

The delicacy of the sense of smell is very remarkable. It has been calculated that even $\frac{3}{1,000,000,0}$ of a grain of musk can be distinctly smelt.

But when the particles issuing from an odoriferous substance are very few, their presence in the air may not be appreciated in normal breathing, because they pass through the respiratory passage only and are not presented to the nerve-endings in the olfactoty region. If under such circumstances a sudden sniff is made, air is forced even into the olfactory tract and the faint odour can be detected.

Even a liberal proportion of odoriferous particles in the air fail making itself felt. For the sense of smell to be excited, the mucous membrane must be neither too dry nor too moist. So When one catches cold his sense of smell is dulled owing to the presence of excessive moisture. There is another reason also why one does not smell properly during cold. The swelling of the mucous membrane covers the nerve filaments rendering them inaccessible to the odoriferous particles.

It is a matter or common experience that perfumes make the strongest impression to start with. Afterwards they grow fainter and even their presence is lost upon us, if we continue long to be in their presence. This circumstance can be accounted for by the fatigue of the sense of smell. The olfactory apparatus is soon exhausted and fails us on that account. If, however, we take a round in the fresh air, the apparatus is refreshed and we can again appreciate the odour.

THE PHARYNX--It has been stated above that the nasal chambers posteriorly open into the throat. These openings are situated above the soft palate and below the base of the cranium. This portion marks the beginning of the pharynx. Now if our reader again looks into the mirror with his mouth widely opened, he will observe that there is something like a wall of flesh covered over with the mucous membrane, stretching behind the tongue and the soft palate. This wall arches above the soft palate in something like a dome. It is exactly under this dome that the posterior openings of the nose are located. Below the tongue the wall descends in the form of a sack that ends in two openings, one of which leads to the aesophagus and the other to the larynx (Vide Fig. 3). From the backward openings of the nasal chambers to the lower openings leading to the aesophagus and the larynx, the same canal stretches continuously and is known as the pharynx. Our reader need not be

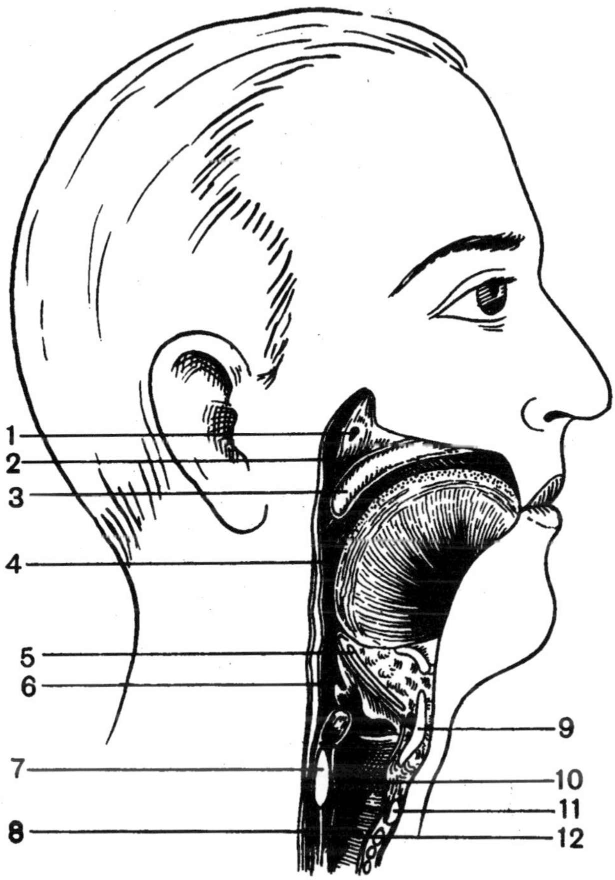

FIG. 3. - The Pharynx Exposed.

(The Tongue is shown below and to the right of the Soft palate)

1 Orifice of the Auditory Tube. 2 Nasal Part of the Pharynx. 3 The Soft Palate. 4 Oral Part of the Pharynx. 5 The Epiglottis. 6 Laryngeal Part of the Pharynx. 7 Cricoid Cartilage. 8 The sophagus. 9 Thyroid Cartilage 10 the Larynx. 11 Cricoid Cartilage. 12 The Trachea

told that the mouth is only an opening in the anterior wall of the pharynx. So upto now we have noticed five openings of the pharynx, two nasal, one oral, one aesophageal and one laryngeal.

There are two more orifices which pierce the pharynx. They are situated in the side walls of the pharynx, one on each side, above the soft palate. They are called *Eustachian orifices,* because they mark the openings of the Eustachian tubes which run to the cavities of the ears. The portion of the pharynx that is situated above the soft palate is called the *nasal part* of the pharynx, that situated behind the mouth and the tongue is called the *oral part*, whereas the remaining portion is called the *laryngeal part.*

The pharynx is used for the passage of the air as it is breathed in and breathed out. In inhalation the air drawn through the nasal cavities passes across the nasal and oral parts of the pharynx and then getting down the larynx goes into the trachea and the lungs. In exhalation the air expelled from the lungs follows the reverse path. At the time of breathing the aesophagus as well as the Eustachian tubes remain closed and the possibility of the air going a wrong way is avoided. Again the soft palate leaves, between it and the back wall of the pharynx, an opening sufficient for free movement of the flowing air. Hence, there is no obstruction in the way of respiration.

At the time of speaking, however, the soft palate completely covers the upper part of the pharynx, so that no air can find its way upward into the nasal part. But in some person, the soft palate is defective, there being a small cleft in it. When these people attempt speaking some of the air from the lungs escapes through this cleft above the palate, and finds its way through the nasal passages that are ever open, adds nasalized element to their voice.

Our reader knows that he uses a part of the pharynx also for swallowing. Food travels through the oral part into the laryngeal pharynx and then gets into the aesophagus. The question is why food going down the pharynx does not run into the larynx and is always pushed down the aesophagus. For this purpose we have to refer to a small organ named epiglottis.

The epiglottis is situated at the root of the tongue (Vide Fig. 3) and serves as cover for the larynx in times of need. In the act of swallowing, the larynx is raised, and the descending morsel lowers the epiglottis which meeting the raised larynx completely covers its mouth. Thus the larynx being closed, food finds its way to the aesophagus or gullet. The rising of the larynx can be felt by anybody by lacing his fingers on the middle of his throat and imitating the act of swallowing. If, however, through mistake even a small particle of food gets the wrong way, we mean gets into the larynx, violent coughing ensues, the system forcibly tries to expel the intruder. Food does not get into the nasal part, because the soft palate completely shuts out that portion during the act of swallowing.

The mucous membrane covering the nose is continuous with the pharynx. It is also to be noted that it continues to cover all the passages leading from the pharynx. It is this circumstance which makes a trouble starting with the throat very often spreads to the nose, the ear and the larynx. That is why running of the nose, deafness of the ear and coughing are on many occasions seen going together.

THE LARYNX---We have noted above that the pharynx has two passages opening from its lower end. They are the aesophagus and the *larynx*. Both the aesophagus and the larynx pass through the neck, the former is situated in the posterior part of it, whereas the latter is situated in the anterior portion. The larynx begins in front of the third cervical vertebra and extends across the fourth, fifth and sixth. The aesophagus starts in front of the sixth cervical. Hence it will be clear that the larynx stands higher up in the neck than the aesophagus. (Vide Fig. 3). As the aesophagus remains constantly closed except at the time of swallowing, the air coming down the pharynx gets into the larynx is always open for this purpose, being closed only during the act of swallowing.

We have already seen that the larynx is situated in the front portion of the neck. There it extends from the base of the tongue downwards. The larynx is a box-like anatomical structure made of different cartilages, and measures less than two inches. Two of these cartilages can be felt even from outside the throat. Starting from the jugular notch upward and feeling the surface of the throat with our fingers, we meet with the first prominence at a short distance. This is the cricoid cartilage. *(Vide Fig. 3).* Travelling further up we come across the next prominence, visibly projecting especially in the case of this persons. This is the thyroid cartilage, the prominence being popularly known as *Adam's apple.* These and other cartilages including the epiglottis which is also a cartilage, are held together by muscles which move them according to the needs of the situation. We have already learnt how the larynx is raised and the epiglottis lowered, during the act of swallowing. As soon as the swallowing is over the larynx is lowered, and the epiglottis raised, leaving the passage free for the air moving to and fro during respiration.

The larynx is popularly known as the voice-box. We want to see now how this box-like instrument is responsible for human voice. Like the pharynx the larynx is covered with mucous membrane on its inner surface, the mucous membrane that covers the pharynx continuing to cover the larynx also. This mucous membrane is thrown into several folds. Two of these start from the front of the box midway in its height, and stretching across its cavity, join the opposite side. These folds are very thin. They are joined together in the front, but are capable of being separated from behind. These folds resituated just behind the thyroid cartilage already referred to. *A* in fig. 4 represents these folds as they stand close together and *C* as they stand wide apart, *B* illustrating the middling position. The three figures indicate the appearance of the folds that they would present to a man peeping into the larynx from above. These folds admit of being brought so tightly together, that they can completely shut up the air below even at a high pressure. These folds are capable of undergoing different degrees of approximation. During normal respiration they stand apart and the passage of the air is smooth and noiseless. But when they are brought close together the air passing through the narrow chink formed by them, throws them into vibrations which in their turn throw the passing air into ripples. It is this rippling air that produces the sound when it strikes our ear. Thus being responsible for the human voice these folds are called *true vocal cords*, the narrow chink between them being called

FIG. 4. - The Vocal Cords.

the *glottis.* These vocal cords are called true because they are to be distinguished from another pair of similar folds situated just above them, which are called *false* vocal cords, because they are not concerned in the production of voice.

The mucous membrane which forms the true vocal cords by forming itself into two this bands, continue to cover the lower portion of the larynx and extends into the trachea into which the larynx opens.

THE TRACHEA-- The trachea or the windpipe is a tube-like anatomical structure some four inches in length. It starts at the bottom of the larynx from behind the cricoid cartilage and extends down into the chest just behind the breastbone. In this persons the upper part of the trachea may be felt with our fingers below the cricoid cartilage. The diameter of the trachea is something like an inch.

The tube of the trachea is formed by cartilaginous rings, from sixteen to twenty in number, which are arranged one above the other, and which are held together by an elastic membrane in which they are enclosed. These rings are not entire but are deficient in part. They are arranged in such a way that the circular part is placed in front and deficient part is placed behind. Of course the deficient part of the tube is covered by the fibrous membrane which clothes the whole trachea. Fig. *5a* represents the appearance of the trachea as seen from the front and Fig. *5b* illustrates the appearance of the same organ as seen from behind.

It has been stated above that the aesophagus is placed just behind the trachea. In fact the membranous part of the trachea and the aesophagus run together. Hence any obstruction in the aesophagus produces a sense of suffocation, although the air passage is free.

A large number of mucous glands is situated in the mucous membrane of the inner surface of the trachea. Under normal conditions the mucous secreted by these glands keeps the passage moist. But if there be an excessive secretion of mucous, it is ejected immediately. The inner mucous membrane of the trachea is lined with ciliated epithelium.[1] These cilia always maintain an upward movement and thus slowly sweep up the secretions towards the larynx from which they are ultimately coughed out.

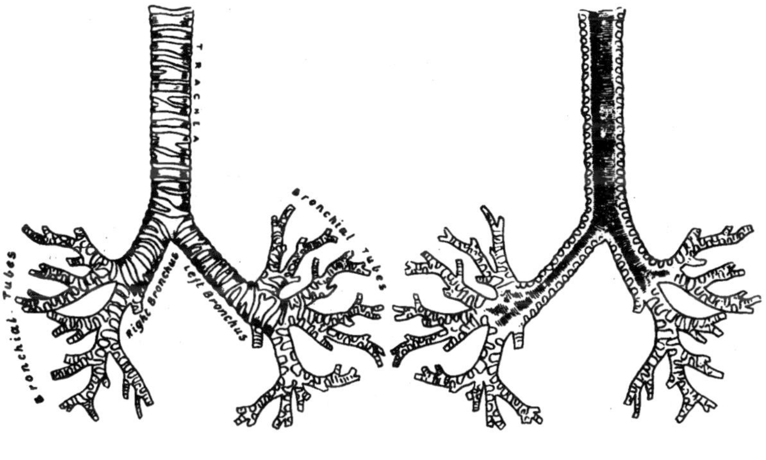

a b

FIG. 5. - TheTrachea and the Bronchial Tubes.

---

1. Epithelium is the delicate tissue forming the outer layer of the mucous membrane. Cilia are very minute hair-like vibrating organs on the surface of the epithelium, forming there a sort of brush.

The Bronchial Tubes -- The trachea when it descends into the chest to the level of the fifth thoracic vertebra, is divided into two tubes called the bronchi. The tube on the left side enters the left lung and is known as the left bronchus, that on the right side entering the right lung being called the *right bronchus*. *(Vide Fig. 5).* After entering into the substance of the lungs, each bronchus divides itself into several branches, these branches again dividing themselves into smaller tubes. These divisions and subdivisions continue to penetrate the substance of the lungs through and through, till at last tubes become so small that their diameter hardly measures 1/40th of an inch. The Trachea with the two bronchi and the numerous smaller and still smaller branches spreading out from them would, if they are separated from the lungs, present the appearance of an inverted tree with the main stalk pointing upward. (*Vide Fig. 5*). When the tubes are reduced to 1/30th of an inch in diameter, they stop subdividing themselves any more. Here the fine bronchial tubes widen themselves and then end in finer air-cells having a diameter of 1/50th of an inch only. A bunch of grapes can very well give a graphic idea of the minute bronchial tubes with air-cells clustering around them. When the air that comes through the nostrils, the pharynx, the larynx, the trachea and the broncial tubes successively, reaches the air-cells, its further passage is stopped. From these cells it is diffused into blood. But before we study this diffusion, we shall note a few important points about these bronchial tubes.

We have seen above that the trachea is made up of cartilaginous rings. Similar cartilaginous portions are present throughout the bronchial tubes except in the last finest branches. The presence of these portions is absolutely for keeping the tubes constantly open for the passage of the air to and from the lungs. Otherwise the tubes would have been exposed to the danger of a collapse.

The fibrous tissue that holds the cartilaginous portions together throughout the length of the bronchial tubes, is very elastic. This circumstance helps the tubes to adopt themselves to the movements of the surrounding anatomical parts.

As in the trachea, so also in the bronchial tubes, the inner mucous membrane is lined with ciliated epithelium. The mucous glands embedded in the mucous membrane, keep their passage moist under healthy circumstances. But in disease when the secretion is excessive, the bronchial tubes stand in danger of being blocked up. Here the cilia try to help the situation. By their perpetual upward movement they work up the secretion up to the larynx. This organ is immediately irritated and throws out the secretion by a cough.

THE LUNGS -- In the previous section we have referred to the air-cells. These air-cells are matted together by means of fibrous tissues. Blood- vessels running through these cells divide and subdivide themselves into myriads of capillaries covering these air-cells. Again there is a network of nerves spreading throughout these structures. All these parts, the cells, the bloodvessels and the nerves form themselves into two masses of a spongy substance each of which is called a lung. We shall now study these statements in greater detail.

Alveoli is another name for the air-cells. All the alveoli developing around themselves a fine bronchial tube, presenting the appearance of a bunch of grapes, go to form what is called an ultimate lobule. Several *ultimate lobules* constitute a lobule and several such lobules are contained in a lobe. The right lung has three such lobes and the left has two. (*Vide Fig. 6*).

The walls of the air-cells which cluster around the finest bronchial tubes, are made of very elastic and circular muscular tissue. The walls are, however, extremely thin, so much so that the air which flows into the cells through the air tubes, is very freely diffused through these walls, although its direct passage is blocked up here.

We have referred to the myriads of capillaries that cover the air-cells. These are the finest ultimate subdivisions of the blood-

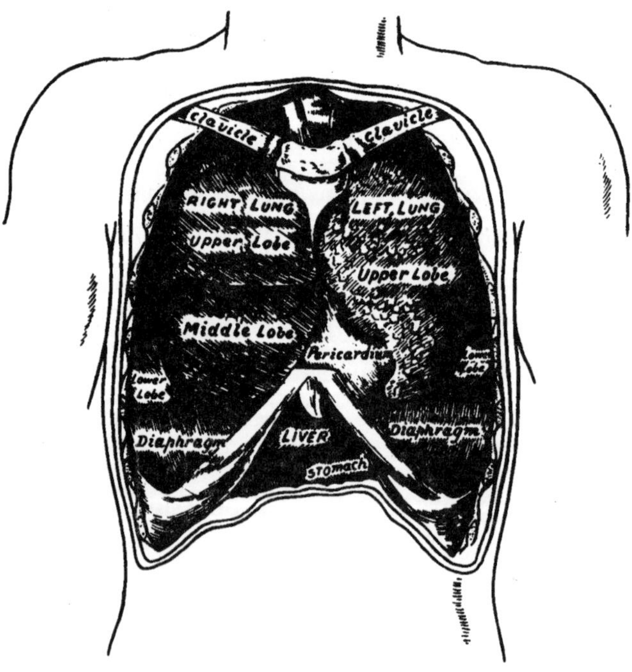

FIG. 6. - The Thorax Exposed.

vessels coming into the lungs and going away from them. The incoming vessels bring impure blood from the heart, to be purified in the lungs. The outgoing vessels carry the purified blood from the lungs back to the heart. Now the network of the capillaries which covers the air-cells is extremely fine, and the walls of the capillaries are extraordinary thin. So when we consider an air-cell, we find that inside the cell there is a stock of fresh air which is surrounded by two extremely thin layers of tissues, the first belonging to the cell and the second pertaining to the capillaries. Beyond these layers is the blood streaming through the capillaries in very fine currents. The two intervening layers, even when put together, are again so thin, that they allow a free interchange between the oxygen from the cells and the carbon dioxide from the capillaries.

The number of blood capillaries which surround the air-cells is so large that it passes all imagination. It is calculated that these capillaries from the two lungs would connect Bombay with London, if they were stretched out in one single line ! We can, however, understand the necessity of this huge length of capillaries, when we know the amount of blood that is presented through them to the air-cells for purification. If the quantity of blood present in the lungs at a particular moment is spread out in a very thin layer, it would cover as many as one thousand square feet at least ! So we find that the arrangement of the air-cells and the capillaries, is to secure a very large surface area for the lungs, within such small limits as the chest of a human being.

This description of the lungs would not be complete unless we explain the two coverings in which the lungs are clothed and which form air-tight bags for holding them. These coverings are called the *pleurae* and consist of a serous membrane, i.e., a smooth glistening membrane that secretes a lubricating fluid. Each lung has a separate pleura of its own, which is folded double, so that the two layers cover the lung completely. Thus an air-tight double bag, having two sheaths one inside the other, of serous membrane is prepared, and each lung is held within this bag. Our reader knows that the lungs are placed inside the thorax. Now the outer layer of the pleura lines the inner surface of the thoracic cavity, and is called the *parietal layer.* The inner layer is adherent to the lungs, and is called the visceral layer.

A tolerably good idea of the relations of the lungs, pleurae and the thorax can be had, if we compare these with a football. The coarse leather bag which forms the outer covering of a football, very well illustrates the rough thorax. Inside this leather cover there is the bladder, a rubber bag which when the ball is to be used is kept inflated. Now, instead of one bladder let us suppose that there are two, one inside the other. When air is pumped into these bags they will swell up. In this inflated condition the outer bag will adhere to the rough leather covering in which these bags are held, and the inner bag will lie closely along the outer rubber bag. The two layers of the pleura lie exactly like the two rubber bags in relation to each other. The only difference is that in the case of the pleural layers there will always be a sort of lubricating fluid secreted by the membrane that allows the two layers to glide smoothly on teach other during the constant movements of respiration. Again in the case of the football, the inside is hollow, whereas in the case of the pleural layers, the inside is filled with the spongy substance of the lungs. Needless to point out that the tube of the rubber bags through which air is pumped in, may clearly illustrate the trachea.

The space between the two layers of the pleurae is called the *pleural cavity*. Under normal conditions of health, the two layers stand so close together, that there is no space left between them. But during inflammatory changes of the membrane, as is pleurisy, the cavity becomes enlarged by an increase in the amount of fluid which it contains.

We have said above that the lungs are held in the thorax. But the lungs are not the only organs situated there. Besides these there are the heart, the big blood-vessels, the trachea and the oesophagus. These are placed between the two pleurae, the right and the left, the cavity in which they are arranged being called the *mediastinal cavity.*

The lungs are short in front and longer behind. In front they descend to the sixth ribs whereas behind they stretch up to the eleventh ribs. This position of the lungs is determined by the position of the diaphragm which forms the floor of the thorax. It is to be remembered that above they rise even a little beyond the clavicles. On an average the right lung weighs 22 ounces in an adult, and the left weigh 20 ounces only.

Thus far we have noticed the different organs through which the air moves, when it passes to and from the lungs during respiration. Now we shall consider the muscular and nervous mechanisms responsible for the movements of these organs of respiration, and shall also study the blood-vessels connected with this function.

The Muscular Mechanism[2]

"The force expended in opening the chest in inspiration each day is enough to raise the person the height[3] of St. Paul's, and is thus only about one-sixth of the force spent in the circulation. Breathing consists of two acts---*inspiration* and *expiration. Inspiration is a forced muscular effort* performed by three distinct sets of muscles--those that act on the ribs, those that act between the ribs, and the diaphragm, which is the floor of the thorax.

"In inspiration the chest cavity is made[4] broader, longer and deeper. When at rest, the ribs, hinged behind to the backbone and in front of the breastbone, hand down like the iron handle on the side of a bucket. (*Vide Fig. 7*). Now, if we raise such a handle, it

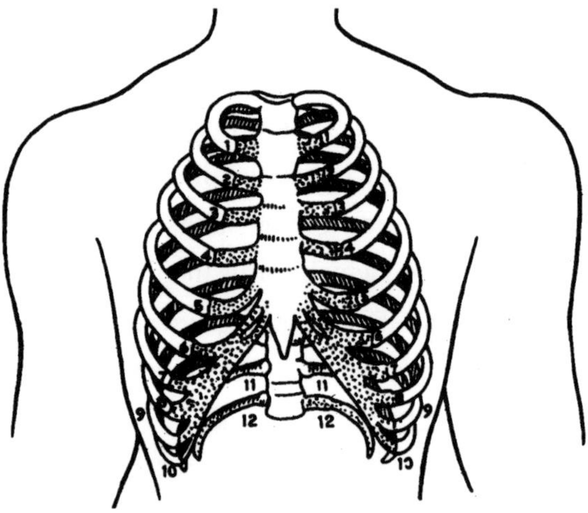

FIG. 7. - The Ribs.
(*The Cartilages have been marked with dots)*

2. In this note, paragraphs included in the quotation marks are extracted from A.T.Schofied's *Articles on Physiology.*
3. Five hundred feet.
4. Increased in the three diameters--lateral, vertical and anteroposterior.

not only moves upward, but also outward. The same takes place with the ribs; and, in addition, the sternum, or breastbone, being movable, rises forward as well, and thus the chest is made *broader and deeper*. It is made longer because, when at rest, the diaphragm muscle forms an arched floor, that rises like a dome into the thorax, and on which the lungs rest. As this muscle contracts it flattens[5] the floor, pulls the lungs down and as a result makes them longer from top to bottom.

"The muscles that raise the ribs are in two sets--those that act on the ribs and those that act between them. The upper ribs are pulled upward by the action of muscles passing down from the neck.

"Between each rib is a double layer of muscles called the intercostal muscles, because they are between the ribs. The top ribs being fixed as these contract, they tend to raise the lower rib, to which they are attached; and thus, by acting together, all the ribs are elevated.

"This constitutes the movement of inspiration.

"In expiration, the chest returns to its *original size* without effort. This is mainly caused by elastic recoil. The lungs are full of elastic tissue which is stretched when the lungs are expanded; and as soon as muscular effort ceases, the elastic force is so great that the lungs pull the ribs down again, and pull up the floor of the diaphragm.

---

5. As has been proved in *Yoga-Mīṃāṃsā* by means of experimental evidence, and as is now held by the medical scientists, the diaphragm does not flatten during contraction, but descends parallel to itself without altering its convexity. Even then the descent of the diaphragm does increase the vertical diameter of the lungs.

"When we draw in a breath the abdomen swells out. This is caused by the contraction of the diaphragm. Which presses all the digestive organs down and makes them bulge out the walls. In expiration the abdomen gets flat again, as the floor rises once more, and the abdominal muscles are contracted.

"The force required to stretch out the elastic tissue in ordinary inspiration is equal to 170 lb; and the total daily force used in respiration is 21 foot-tons".[6]

In extraordinary or forced breathing the force required for the act is much more than in normal respiration. Both in inhalation and exhalation additional muscles are brought into play. The additional muscles which are called into action in forced inspiration are situated in the neck and chest. In forced expiration the abdominal muscles play a very important part.

It is to be especially borne in mind that speaking, singing, blowing etc., are voluntary expiratory efforts, whereas sneezing, coughing etc., are involuntary. In all these action the abdominal muscles are brought specially into action.

When one holds his breath after inhalation all the muscles of inspiration remain contracted and the glottis is tightly closed. So also it remains tightly closed when one holds his breath after deep exhalation. At this time, however, it is the muscles of expiration that maintain their full contraction.

It is to be noted here that the air outside freely communicates

---

6. Force required to raise one ton of weight through twenty-one feet against gravity, or to raise twenty-one tons of weight through one foot against gravity.

with the lungs when the glottis is open. We have noted above that glottis remains closed only at the time of swallowing. So during all the twenty-four hours of the day, the air outside communicates freely with the lungs. Now this outside air always stands at an atmospheric pressure, and if it gets communication with a space that stands at a lower pressure, it will flow to that space till the pressure outside that space and inside it becomes equalized. This is exactly what happens at the time of inspiration. When the lungs become broader, deeper and longer owing to the opening up of the chest, the pressure inside the lungs is lowered and the outside air rushes in through the trachea till internal pressure becomes equal to that of the atmosphere. This constitutes the act of inspiration.

It has been stated in the foregoing paragraphs that in inspiration the ribs are elevated and the diaphragm sinks, pressing the abdominal viscera, thus leading to the bulging out of the abdomen. When the whole muscular mechanism of respiration is healthy, the rising of the ribs and the bulging out of the abdomen are proportionate. But in case of defective respiratory mechanism, either the abdominal movement or the costal movement is more prominent than the other. This circumstance has led to a distinction in the types of breathing. That respiration in which the costal movement is prominent, is called *costal breathing.* Again the breathing in which the abdominal movement is more in evidence, is called *abdominal breathing or diaphragmatic breathing.* The latter breathing bears a double name because the abdominal movements depend upon the movements of the diaphragm.

Due to old age or disease the chest becomes rigid. Under these circumstances the breathing becomes abdominal. People very often, due to their peculiarities of dress, make the movement of the abdomen almost impossible. If this habit is continued over a long time, breathing becomes costal rather than abdominal. Owing to these reasons it is desirable that the whole mechanism of respiration is allowed the greatest scope for movement.

When the chest begins to sink, the pressure inside the lungs is increased and becomes greater than the pressure outside the lungs. Hence air is driven out of the lungs through the trachea, till at last the elastic recoil is completed and again the internal and external pressures are equalized. This constitutes the act of expiration.

Whatever the amount of air inside the lungs either during inspiration or expiration, that air exerts an equal pressure on each of the lungs as a whole; and keeps it, under all conditions, closely in contact with the walls and the floor of the chest.

The number of respiration under conditions is between fourteen and twenty per minute.

Having noted the muscular mechanism of respiration, we now proceed to study the nervous mechanism of it.

The Nervous Mechanism

The respiratory centre is a nervous mechanism situated at the posterior part of the brain, almost at its lower end. The centre is responsible for controlling the activities of the muscles that cause inspiration and expiration. This central control is both voluntary and involuntary.

Practically our breathing is under our own control up to the point where life is involved. We can breathe in any manner and at any rate we please. Were it not so, speaking would become impossible. We can also hold our breath up to a certain points; but when life is beginning to be threatened the voluntary control comes to an end, and in spite of the strongest effort of will, forces us to breath. The involuntary control also acts continuously when we are not thinking of our breath at all. None of the vital processes require our constant attention; yet with some we are allowed to play up to the point of danger but not further.

We shall refer to this nervous mechanism again at the end of this chapter.

The Quantity Air We Breathe

The quantity of air we breathe depends upon the depth of respiration. In the ordinary normal respiration, the quantity of air that uniformly flows in is about 500 ml. (milli-litre). As much air also flows out during normal expiration. Thus the volume of the tide of air that constantly and uniformly flows in and our is about 500 ml. This is called tidal air and the volume of such air is called tidal volume.

But if the inspiration were to be deeper, it is obvious that a larger quantity of air will be drawn in. It is estimated that about 2500 ml. of air can be drawn in by an average adult in the deepest inspiration This is called the inspiratory capacity and includes tidal volumc.

Again as average adult can expel about 1300 ml. of air by a forcible deep expiration over and above the 500 ml. which he expels in his normal exhalation. The additional air expelled by a forcible deep expiration is called expiratory reserve volume.

It is to be noted, however, that even the deepest expiration will not be able to empty the air-cells completely. There will always be a reside of air left in the lungs. This residue is calculated to be equal to 1600 ml. (milli litres) and is called residual volume.

At the end of a quiet respiration the lungs contain the expiratory reserve volume and the residual capacity (2900 ml.).

The amount of air breathed in per minute is called the respiratory minute-volume or pulmonary ventilation. Since the respiratory rate at rest is about 16 per minute and the tidal volume 500 ml., the minute volume is about 8 litres. In exercise it may go up to 70 litres.

We shall refer to this nervous mechanism again at the end of this chapter.

Upto now we have seen how we breathe and also how much we breathe. Now we will see why we breathe at all.

Why We Breathe

A solution to this problem is available in the comparison of the quality of the air we breathe in and quality of the air we breathe out. Roughly speaking, the following is the composition[7] of the two types of air : -

PER HUNDRED POINTS

	Nitrogen	oxygen	Carbon Dioxide
Inspired Air	79	20.96	0.04
Expired Air	79	16.02	4.38
		-4.94	+4.34

7. Only those constituents that are important from the physiological standpoint have been compared here.

Here we at once find that the expired air has lost 4.94 parts of oxygen and has gained 4.34 parts of carbon dioxide in going into and coming out of the lungs. Where has this oxygen gone and whence has this carbon dioxide come ? Oxygen has been taken up by the stream of blood that circulates through the lung capillaries and carbon dioxide has been substituted for it by the same agency.

If we bring together two vessels containing two different gases without any partition between them, the two gases will mix up thoroughly. This very thing happens even if the two gases were to be separated by a thin partition of a membrane. Now we know that the blood streaming through the capillaries around the air-cells and the air in the air-cells, are separated only by a thin partition consisting of the walls of the capillaries and the air-cells. So the gases of the air and the blood mix up freely. This is what is called the *diffusion of gases.* In the figures quoted above for comparison, we find that the quantity of oxygen substituted for carbon dioxide, is greater than the quantity of carbon dioxide by 0.60. This is because oxygen is used not only in forming carbon dioxide, but also for some other physiological work.

Now we proceed to see why the circulating blood current the lung capillaries, wants to borrow oxygen and tries to lose carbon dioxide.

In this connection we are to remember that the human body is constantly at work even when apparently it is at rest. The circulatory system, the respiratory system, the digestive system etc., know no rest. They have to work ceaselessly. This perpetual work means constant wear and tear of the body tissues involved in the work. So the loss of the tissues is to be made good and waste products are to be removed and thrown out of the body. Now for making good the loss, nourishment has to be brought to these tissues. This nourishment is derived not only from food and drink, but also from the inspired air in the form of oxygen. Why oxygen form the most important factor of nourishment. We cannot live without oxygen even few minutes. So when the blood comes to the lungs, it borrows oxygen from the inspired air and carries it to the different parts of the body through the circulatory system. Again the blood when it comes to the lungs is full of carbon dioxide collected from the tissues all over the body. It is a waste product resulting from the working of the bodily machine. If this gas is allowed to remain in the system, it would poison the body. Hence it has to be got rid of. The inspired air is poorer in carbon dioxide. Hence it is willing to borrow the same from the blood and take it away with expiration.

We now understand why we breathe. We breathe in order to absorb oxygen and to throw away carbon dioxide, both the processes being absolutely essential for the life of a human being.

The venous blood when it absorbs oxygen and gets rid of carbon dioxide, is said to be arterialized. Venous blood is first collected in the heart and hence is pushed into the lungs. There it is arterialized and again sent back to the heart to be distributed to the different parts of the body and to be returned again to the heart as venus blood.[8]

---

8. For details of the circulatory system, readers are referred to our note on that system given in *Yoga-Mīṃāṃsa,* Vol. I. It appears there under the heading "A Few Facts About the Blood and Blood Circulation".

The venous blood is purple because of carbon dioxide and the arterialized blood is bright scarlet because of its oxygen. This can be proved by experimentation. If a quantity of the venous blood is put into a bottle containing oxygen and shaken, it will turn bright scarlet. On the contrary if the arterial blood is put into a bottle containing carbon dioxide and shaken, it will turn purple.

We undertook to revert to the nervous mechanism of respiration at the end of this chapter. What we now want to say in that connection is this:

The quantity of oxygen and carbon dioxide and especially of the latter present in the blood, has been discovered to have great influence upon the respiratory centre. If the quantity of carbon dioxide present in the blood goes beyond its normal measure, the respiratory centre at once becomes more active and respirations become rapid. This is best seen when a man is taking hard muscular exercise. On the contrary the centre is calmed down if the quantity of carbon dioxide present in the blood falls below its normal measure with the result that respiration becomes slower than usual. Although the most important factor in the regulation of respiration is the quantity of carbon dioxide in the blood passing through the respiratory centre, the impulses reaching this centre from the carotid body, the carotid sinus and the sinus nerve are also responsible for changing the activity of the respoiratory centre. For understanding the effects of these impulses, read Jālandharabandha (Chapter II).

CHAPTER II

ĀSANAS APPROPRIATE TO PRĀṆĀYĀMA

(Note -- Two Dṛṣṭis and three Bandhas are a part of the technique of the meditative poses. We begin this chapter with a description of these Dṛṣṭis and Bandhas, with a view to enable our readers to follow the technique of the Āsanas without any interruption.)

NĀSĀGRA-DṚṢṬI OR THE NASAL GAZE

FIXING one's eyes upon one's tip of the nose is called Nāsāgra Dṛṣṭi in Sanskrit. Nāsāgra means the tip of the *nose* and Dṛṣṭi means gaze. It is illustrated in Fig.8. It may be practised as a part of Padmāsana[1] or independent of it. In the accompanying picture, the head is thrown back a little with a view to make the position of the eyeballs visible.

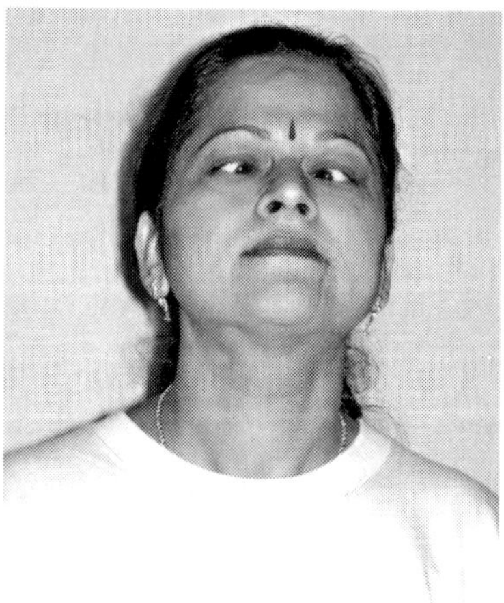

FIG. 8. -Nāsāgra Dṛṣṭi or the Nasal Gaze.

1. Described later on in this chapter.

The Nasal Gaze is a fine exercise for the wandering mind. Its practice if undertaken with zest and carried over a period of some months continuously, has a perceptibly beneficial effect on the unsteady mind.

Caution -- The Nasal Gaze directly works upon the brain through the optic nerves. Everybody should, therefore, develop this gaze very slowly and cautiously. Persons with weak nerves are warned not to undertake this practice except under supervision.

BHRŪMADHYA-DṚṢṬI OR THE FRONTAL GAZE

Fixing one's eyes between the eyebrows is called Bhrūmadhya-Dṛṣṭi in Sanskrit. Bhrūmadhya means the *space between the eyebrows*. It is illustrated in Fig. 9. It may be practised as a part of Siddhāsana[2] or independent of it.

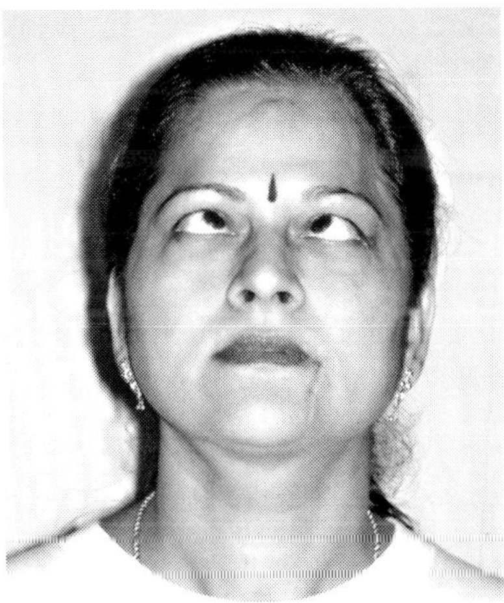

FIG. 9. - Bhrūmadhya Dṛṣṭi of the Frontal Gaze

2. Described later on in this chapter.

Like the Nasal Gaze, the Frontal Gaze is a fine exercise for the mind. But the advice and caution given in the case of the former are equally applicable to the case of the latter. Hence they should be carefully borne in mind by the enthusiastic student of Yoga.

UḌḌIYĀNA-BANDHA OF THE RAISING OF THE DIAPHRAGM

Uḍḍiyāna is an exercise of the diaphragm and the ribs. When expressed in a popular[3] language its technique may be described as follows.

As this Bandha is practised either in sitting or in standing posture, the student poses himself as shown in Figs. 10 and 12

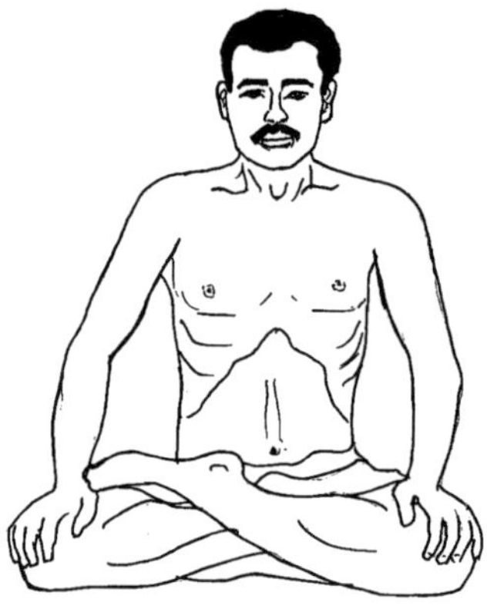

FIG. 10. - Uḍḍiyāna in Sitting.

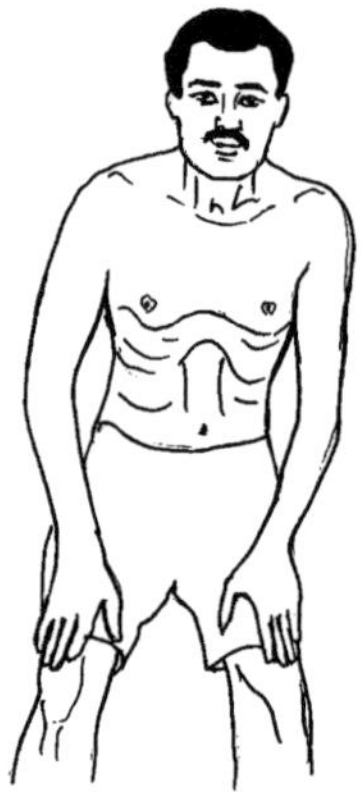

FIG. 12. - Uḍḍiyāna in Standing.

3. This Bandha has been subjected by us to a very large number of X-ray and other experiments, many of which have already appeared in Yoga-Mīṃāṃsā. Hence we are in a position to give a detailed scientific description of its technique. Looking to the popular character of this publication, however, we have sketched its technique in the simplest terms possible.

respectively. In these pictures, hands are shown to be resting either on the knees or on the thighs. This position of the hands enables them to be firmly pressed against their support and thus to fix upon the muscles of the neck and the shoulders. Having taken this posture the student secures the deepest possible expiration by vigorously contracting the front muscles of the abdomen. The chest also stands contracted. While the breath is held out, the muscles of the neck and the shoulders are fixed up by firmly pressing the hands either against the knees or against the thighs as the case may be. Then a vigorous mock inhalation is attempted by raising the ribs and by not allowing the air to flow into the lungs. Simultaneously the front abdominal muscles are completely relaxed.

The fixing up of the neck and shoulders, the vigorous mock inhalation preceded by the deepest possible exhalation, and the simultaneous relaxation of the contracted front abdominal muscles, these three actions complete the technique of Uḍḍiyāna. Automatically[4] the diaphragm will rise upon and the abdomen will undergo a pronounced depression, producing the concave appearance shown in Figs. 11 and 12. A slight forward bent of the trunk will be helpful in securing greater abdominal concavity of Uḍḍiyāna.

---

4. The pressure changes in the chest and abdomen which are responsible for this automatic abdominal depression, have been detailed in Yoga-Mīmāṃsā in places too numerous to be quoted here. Zealous students of Yogic physiology may read the *Scientific Sections* of Vols. III and IV of the journal.

FIG. 11. - Uḍḍiyāna Bandha in Sitting (*Side View)*

When the student finds that he can no longer hold his breath out comfortable, he relaxes his neck and shoulders, lets go the ribs and slowly starts inhalation, allowing the abdominal depression to be effected gradually. When inhalation is completed, one round of the Uḍḍiyāna exercise is finished.

In Sanskrit, Uḍḍiyāna means raising up and Bandha means *contraction of particular anatomical parts.* This exercise is called Uḍḍiyāna-Bandha because the muscular contractions described above enable the spiritual force[5] to rise up. Anatomically this Bandha may be called Uḍḍiyāna because it raises the diaphragm.

Uḍḍiyāna is a very fine exercise for the abdomen. Its therapeutical value against constipation, dyspepsia, liver troubles, etc., is very great. Its spiritual worth is greater still.

---

5. This force is locked up in the lower region of the abdomen. Uḍḍiyāna is one of the different exercises capable of letting loose this force and making it travel upward along the spine.

Caution -- People suffering from circulatory or serious abdominal troubles should not take to this exercise on their own responsibility.

JĀLANDHARA-BANDHA OR THE CHIN-LOCK

कण्ठमाकुञ्च्य हृदये स्थापयेत् चिबुकं दृढम् । H. P. III-70
बन्धो जालंधराख्यः अयं जरामृत्युविनाशकः ।।
बध्नाति हि सरोजालम् आधोगामि नभोजलम् ।
ततो जालंधरो बन्धः .... H. P. III-71

(kaṇṭhamākuñcya hṛdaye sthāpayert cibukarṃ dṛḍham/
bandho jālandharākhyaḥ ayaṃ jarāmṛtyuvināśkaḥ)
(bandhnāti hi sirojālarn adhogāmi nabhaojalm/
tato jālandharo bandhaḥ............)

Translation

After contracting the throat (one) should tightly fix the chin on the chest. The name of this Bandha is Jālandhara. (Fig. 14 and 15). It prevents old age and death. It is called Jālandhara because it presses on the arteries going to the brain and also arrests the downward flow of nectar issuing from it.

The Name

In Yoga literature Bandha which literally means a *tie* is a word applied to various muscular contractions and relaxations that are expected to influence the vascular nervous and the glandular systems. When we presently discuss the technique of Bandha, we will find that it influences the arteries supplying blood to the brain and also presses on a particular nerve having various physiological effects.

FIG. 14. - Jalandhara-Bandha or the Chin-Lock (*Front View*)

FIG. 15. - Jālandhara-Bandha or the Chin-Lock (*Side view*)

The Technique

When it is said that the throat is to be contracted, what is intended really is the closure of the two vocal cords which are situated in the larynx. A reference to Fig. 3 will show the position of the larynx. We have to close these cords when we hold our breath. Along with the closure of the glottis which means the open space between the two cords, one has also to tighten muscles of the neck. One then bends his head as best as he can and presses his chin on the chest as firmly as possible. In short this is the technique of this Bandha.

Jālandhara may be practised at any stage of the respiratory movement. But in Ābhyantara Prāṇāyāma it is to be effected after deep inhalation except in Mūrcha Prāṇāyāma where its continuation is advised even during Recaka. Of course during this Recaka the vocal cods will have to be slight relaxed.

Anatomy and Physiology of Jālandhara

It will require a large number of laboratory experiments carried through years and years before the physiological and psychophysiological effects of Jālandhara are scientifically investigated. These effects are so vast and varied. We will, therefore, satisfy ourselves here with a few observations which are known to modern physiology and apply them to Jālandhara. This effort will, however, be sufficient to understand the main physiological effects of this Bandha.

For this physiological study we have to take into account certain anatomical structures. They are (1) The Internal and external carotid arteries, (2) The carotid sinus, and (3) The sinus nerve. We shall consider them one by one regarding their location, structure etc.

(1) The internal and external carotid arteries : A reference to Fig. 13 will show that these arteries lie in the neck and are branches of the common carotid. These two arteries mainly responsible for bringing blood supply to the brain. They are situated on both the sides of the neck. If we throw back our head and put our thumb on the right side of the neck just below the jaw-bone and the forefinger similarly on the left side, we will feel the pulsation of these arteries.

(2) The carotid sinus is a dilatation present at the bifurcation of the common carotid artery Fig. 13. It is usually restricted to the first part of the internal carotid. The walls of this sinus are so thin, that they yield very easily to the pressure applied to it either internally or externally.

(3) The sinus nerve is a branch of a cranial nerve coming from the brain. Rising below the skull it descends on the internal carotid artery and is distributed to the wall of the carotid sinus. The sinus nerve is a presso-receptor, that means, a nerve which is stimulated

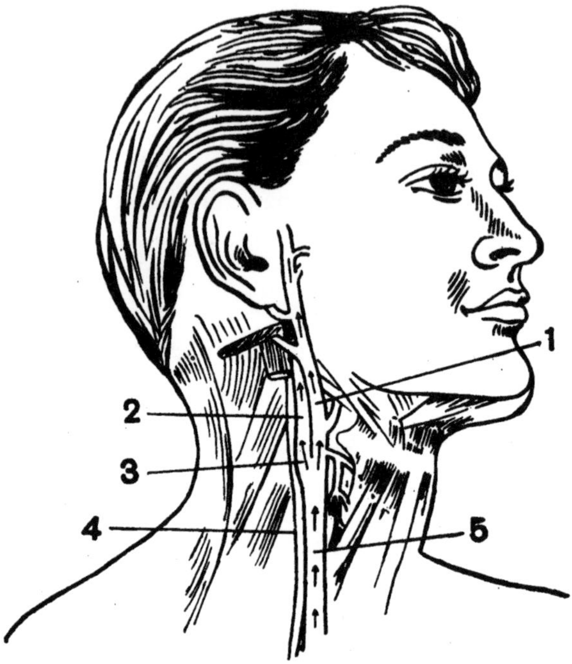

Fig. 13. - The Carotids Exposed
(1) The External Carotid (2) The Internal Carotid (3) The Carotid Sinus (4) The Vagus Nerve (5) The Common Carotid

by internal or external pressure. In the case of the sinus nerve the external pressure can be applied to it by pressing the carotid sinus by using the thumb and the forefinger as stated under (2) above

After noting a few anatomical points, we now study the physiology of this Bandha.

If pressure is applied externally to the carotid sinus, the sinus nerve is stimulated and nerve impulses travelling to the brain bring about a condition that cannot be distinguished from sleep. According to some physiologists a genera trance-like is induced in the brain. This stimulation also slows down the heart.

The physiological phenomena described in the last paragraph were known to the old Yogins. For inducing loss of awareness and ultimately to realise the blissful and pure Brahman, they advised this very stimulation of the carotid nerve. Their name for this nerve was विज्ञाननाडी (vijñānanāḍī), that is, the nerve of consciousness. We quote in this connection Śiva Saṃhitā, line V-55 and 56 here which are as follows :

विज्ञाननाडीद्वितयम् अङ्गुलीभ्यां निरोधयेत् ।। V-55
सिद्धे तदाविर्भवति सुखरूपी निरञ्जनः । V-56

(vijñānanāḍīdvitayam aṅgulībhyāṃ nirodhayet)
(siddhe tadavirbhavati sukharūpī nirañjanaḥ)

When translated this would stand in the following form.

(The Yogin) should press with his two fingers the two carotid nerves (on the two sides of the neck). When (this practice) is perfected, blissful and pure Brahman reveals itself.

Now in the case of Jālandhara, the closure of the glottis, the tightening of the neck muscles and the sharp bend of the neck in pressing the chin on the chest, all contribute to exercise considerable pressure on the carotid sinus, so that the carotid nerve gets stimulated. When by constant practice this Bandha is perfected, its effect on the brain becomes accentuated and a trance-like condition may supervene. It is to be noted that in some person the carotid nerve is so sensitive that even a slight pressure may wipe out consciousness and also slow down the heart. When Jālandhara is maintained, not only in Kumbhaka but also in Recaka, it should bring about stupor as is claimed in Mūrchā Prāṇāyāma.

For achieving the results stated in the Śiva Saṃhitā 'विज्ञाननाडी निरोध' is to be practised with concentration and for months and years.

Some Technical Considerations

In discussing the technique of different Prāṇāyāma we have advised students not to Practise Kumbhaka without Jālandhara. This advice is given for the following reasons.

When breath is held for a long time after deep inhalation the air inhaled has a strong tendency to rush out. Even if the glottis is kept closed, it is forced open under pressure of the pent up air and elastic recoil of the lungs. The result is that the air rushes through the eustachian or auditory tubes to the internal ear and leads to various disorder. These tubes start in the pharynx Fig. 3 and lead to the internal ear. They remain closed ordinarily, but open owing to the rushing air, if the mouth is closed as is generally done during Prāṇāyāma and particularly during Kumbhaka. Jālandhara because of the tightening of the whole throat and the sharp bend of the neck prevents the onrush of the air, even if the vocal cords give way and the glottis is opened. So no doubt the closure of the glottis is the first line of defence against any mischief to the ear due to Kumbhaka but Jālandhara serves as the second line of defence. It is always desirable to be doubly protected.

MŪLA-BANDHA OR THE ANAL CONTRACTION

Mūla-Bandha is an exercise which mainly consists in forcibly contracting the anal sphincters. It also requires the perineum to be closely pressed by the heel, as illustrated in Fig. 18 and as described later on in this chapter in the technique of Siddhāsana.

Mūla-Bandha may be practised as a part of Siddhāsana or independent of it.

There are two anal sphincters, one internal and the other external, situated at the end of the rectum. Both are formed by circular muscles, the external sphincter constituting the anus.

Although the anal contraction alone goes to form Mūla-Bandha, in contracting the anus one necessarily contracts the whole pelvic region. Hence virtually Mūla-Bandha is an exercise of pelvic contraction.

This Mūla-Bandha is intended to work upon the central and sympathetic nervous systems through the nerve terminal in the anal sphincters. It is called Mūla-Bandha because it first concerns itself with the lower ends of the nervous system in the human trunk.

Caution -- A mistake in the practice of this Bandha leads to hard constipation and upsets the digestive system. The genitals are also involved in this direction and a mistake in its execution may result in some trouble in that direction also. Hence students of Yoga are advised to proceed systematically into this practice.

PADMĀSANA OR THE LOTUS POSE

This pose is called Padmāsana because it is imitation of the lotus that the hands and feet are arranged in this Āsana. Padma, in Sanskrit, means a lotus. Possibly the two feet placed on the opposite thighs represent the lotus leaves, and the two hands arranged one above the other stand for the blooming lotus. Fig. 17 illustrates the full pose.

The student first takes his seat with his legs fully stretched out. He then bends his right leg in the knee-joint and folding it upon itself, sets the same in the opposite hip-joint, so as to make the foot lie stretching at the root of the thigh with its sole upturned. (Vide Fig. 16). The other leg is similarly folded and set in the opposite hip-joint. He adjusts both the heels in such a way that they almost meet in front of the pubic bones and each of them presses on the abdominal portion adjacent to it. (Vide Fig. 17). Then on the heels thus brought together, the left hand is spread out with its back touching the heels and its palm upturned. The right hand is placed upon the left in the same manner. The eyes are directed to the nose-tip as described on p. 23 and the Chin-Lock is formed after the manner indicated on pp. 25, 26. With the Anal Contraction treated on p. 29 the technique of the Lotus Pose is completed. It is needless to add that except for the neck, the spine is to be maintained erect.

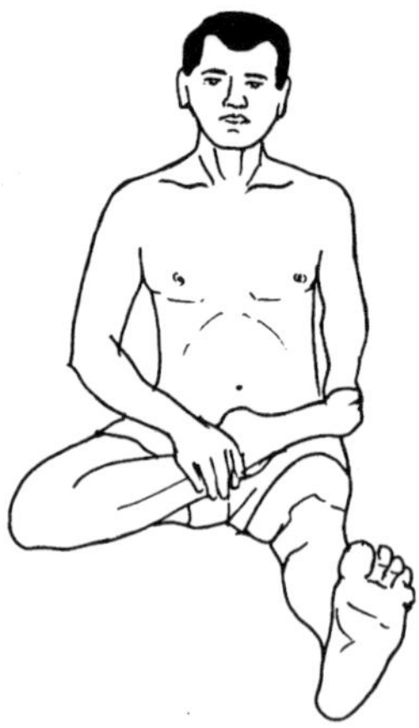

FIG. 16. - Preparation of Padmāsana

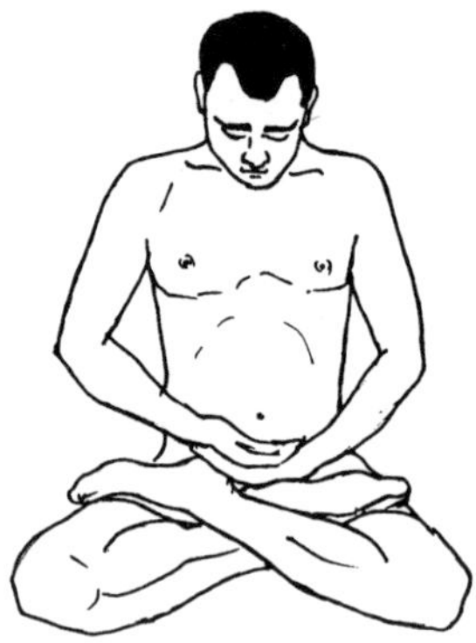

FIG. 17. - Padmāsana or the Lotus Pose.

The most important features of Prāṇāyāma are the two Bandhas-Jālandhara and Mūla. As these are to be cautiously practised, it is always desirable, for the student of Yoga, first to pick up the Bandhas and then start with this pose.

Caution -- In India many people are desirous of sitting in Padmāsana for their daily prayers. We advise these people to assume the Lotus Pose without the Bandhas, If they have not already picked them up successfully. When practised without Bandhas, this, Āsana may be continued for any length of time, provided one can sit in it all the while without any sense of discomfort. The advice and caution given in the notes on these Bandhas, also hold good in the case of Prāṇāyāma. If the student is anxious to go through the complete techniques of this posture.

SIDDHĀSANA OR THE ACCOMPLISHED POSE

The pose is called Siddhāsana because it is a favourite of the accomplished Yogins Siddha, in Sanskrit, means an *adept.*

The student first taks his seat with his legs fully stretched out. He then bends his left leg in the knee-joint and folding it upon itself, sets its heel tightly against the perineum. (Vide Fig. 18). In order to get the perineum clear for his purpose, he has first to hold up his genitals with the left hand, for the right hand is occupied in setting the heel in its proper place. The sole of the left foot

FIG. 18. - Preparation for Siddhāsana.

should be closely in touch with the right thigh. No attempt should be made to sit on the heel. This is a wrong procedure, because pressure is to be exerted on the perineum and not on the anus. The adjusted heel should feel the hard touch of the bones on the two sides of the perineum. After the left leg is given its proper position, the genitals should be arranged within the space available between the left thigh and the left calf. This being done the right leg should be folded after the manner of the left, its heel being placed against the pubic bones just above the penis. (Vide Fig. 19). The right sole should spread along the left thigh, the lower border of the right foot being thrust between the left thigh and the left calf. Care must be taken not to hurt the genitals. Generally they can be accommodated below the right heel. But if they cannot find sufficient space there, the testes may be lodged there and the penis may be made to lie outside the folded legs. Under no circumstances should undesirable pressure be put upon any of the organs concerned.

FIG. 19. - Siddhāsana or the Accomplished Pose.

The chin is set against the chest, just in Padmāsana, to form Jālandhara-Bandha. The eyes, this time, do not, however, gaze at the tip of the nose but are directed between the eyebrows, as described on p. 23 securing Bhrūmadhya-Dṛṣṭi for the student. Except for this bend of the neck the spine is to be erect.

The hands and fingers may be arranged as shown in Fig. 19 or the hands may rest on the knees, touching them with their palms.

The pose should be developed gradually avoiding every possibility of uncomfortable pressure. The period of time given its daily practice should increase slowly.

Note -- In some of the vernacular books on Yoga, the pose is said to affect the sexual power adversely. So far as our experience goes, there is little evidence in support of this view, in the case of healthy persons. It is however, desirable not to exceed an hour's practice, without special permission of an expert.

This and the preceding Āsana are principally practised for spiritual culture. When rightly advised they are also available for purposes of physical culture and therapeutics.

SVASTIKĀSANA OR THE AUSPICIOUS POSE

This pose is called Svastikāsana because it involves crossing of the legs which is looked upon by the Āryans as auspicious. In Sanskrit, Svastika means *auspicious.* In classical Sanskrit the word Svastika is used even for the *crossing of the hands.* The reason is that the mysterious symbol Svastika is mainly represented by two lines crossing each other at right angles. Hence positions involving the crossing either of hands or of legs are also called Svastika. Fig. 21 which illustrates Svastikāsana, clearly shows how in this Āsana legs cross each other above the ankles.

The student starts by stretching out his legs on his seat. Then he bends one of his legs, say the right, in the knee, and folds it on the thigh, just as in the case of Siddhāsana. But there is a difference in the ultimate position of the foot in this pose and in Siddhāsana. In the latter pose the heel is set against the perineum, whereas in Svastikāsana it is to be set against the opposite groin, so as to allow the corresponding sole to be in close touch with the opposite thigh. (*Vide* Fig. 20). Then without disturbing the position of the heel, the student raises the toes of his right leg with his left hand. Simultaneously he folds his left leg upon the thigh in such a way that the big toe of his right and leg may project itself above the calf and the thigh between which it is held, and the left heel may be firmly set against the right groin. The toes of the left foot are inserted between the right calf and the right thigh already folded upon each other, allowing only the big left toe to lie free. (*Vide* Fig. 21). Needless to say that in this position the sole of the left foot stretches above the right thigh touching it closely all along. In this pose the legs should be made to cross each other just above the ankles, so that all unpleasant pressure on the bones will be avoided. When the legs are properly adjusted a sort of foot lock is prepared which one finds very comfortable, and capable of being maintained for a considerable length of time.

The spine is to be kept erect. No attempt is, however, to be made to throw out the chest. Svastikāsana is a meditative pose

FIG. 20. - Preparation for Svastikāsana.

FIG. 21. - Svastikāsana or the Auspicious Pose.

and as such requires to be maintained for a long time. Any attempt to give an artificial bend to the vertebral column is likely to involve a strain.

The arms may hang loosely from the shoulders and rest on the knees covering them with their palms. Or they may be stretched out a little further so as to rest the wrist on the corresponding knees. In the latter case the hands are formed into what is called Jñāna-Mudrā[6] in Yoga. Fig. 21 illustrates the full pose.

A third way of arranging the hands is shown in Padmāsana. (*Vide* Fig. 17).

Instead of starting with the right leg, the student may start with the left. He might then go through the whole technique, introducing corresponding changes throughout.

The eyes may either be closed as illustrated in Fig. 21 or either the Nasal Gaze or the Frontal Gaze may be practised. (For the two Dṛṣṭis see respectively Figs. 8 and 9).

All over the lower extremities the flexors are greatly contracted and pressed.

This circumstance coupled with the passive condition of all the muscles of the lower extremities maintained for a considerably long time, interfers with the free current of blood circulation. That being the case, the pelvic region gets a larger blood supply from the bifurcations of the abdominal aorta.

---

6. The technique of this is given in the next chapter under the subheading 'Mudrā.'

The larger blood supply mentioned above tones up the coccygeal and sacral nerves.

SAMĀSANA OR THE SYMMETRICAL POSE

This pose is called Samāsana because in its performance all the parts of the human body are symmetrically arranged and a perfect balance maintained. In Sanskrit, Sama means *symmetrical.*

Guptāsana is another name given to this pose. In Sanskrit Gupta means either well *protected or secret.* The pose looks to be called Guptāsana because in executing it, genitals are well protected under the heels of man. Or it may be that the Āsana was practised secretly by a particular school Yogins and continued to be their secret possession, till it became known to others and hence acquired this name.

The only difference in the technique of this Āsana and the previous one, lies in the arrangement of the heels. In Svastikāsana the right heel is pressed against the opposite groin and also the left. But the Samāsana the right and the left heels are to be set against the pubic one, that is, the bone just above the penis. This is done as follows. While the right leg is being folded on the corresponding thigh, the student holds the heel in his right hand and the toes in his left. Then he turns the heel upward and the toes downward, and arranges the foot in his front in such a way that the heel presses against the pubic bones, the sole is turned up, and the upper surface of the foot touches the ground. (*Vide* Fig. 22) Care must be taken at this time to see that the genitals are paced the heel in such a way that no pressure is exerted on the testes. The other leg is similarly folded and the other heel is placed upon

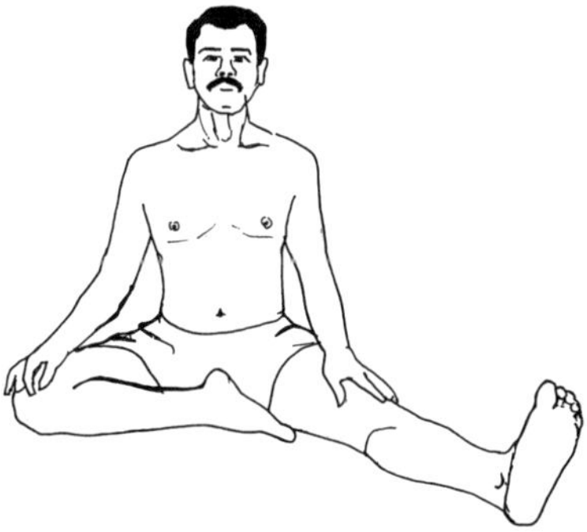

FIG. 22. - Preparation for Samāsana.

FIG. 23. - Samāsana or the Symmetrical Pose.

the first heel, pressing against the pubic bone. The toes of the other leg are to be inserted between the calf and thigh of the first leg. (*Vide* Fig. 23).

The arrangement of the hands and eyes in this Āsana admits of as many varieties as in the previous Āsana. The spine is to be maintained erect and the whole body to be kept in balance.

So far as could be observed up to now from the physiological point of view, Samāsana seems to have the same effect upon the muscles, blood-vessels and nerves as Svastikāsana.

Note -- As in this pose the space below the heels is just sufficient to accommodate genitals of the normal size, persons who are suffering from hydrocele etc., should not attempt this Āsana.

CHAPTER III

PRĀṆĀYĀMA IN GENERAL

Place of Prāṇāyāma in Yogic Curriculum

THE course of Yogic study is divided into eight parts. Āsana constitutes the third part. A student of Yoga passes on to Prāṇāyāma after mastering Āsana. In the present chapter we propose to treat this fourth item of the Yogic curriculum in general, details of the different types of Prāṇāyāma being reserved for separate chapters that follow. Again in the present Chapter we shall first give a general idea about Prāṇāyāma and then discuss a few technicalities common to all varieties of Prāṇāyāma.

Meaning of Prāṇāyāma

Prāṇāyāma[1] means a *pause in the movement of breath.* In Sanskrit Prāṇa- means *breath* and Āyāma means a pause. In modern literature on Yoga, Prāṇa, even in the compound Prāṇāyāma, has

---

1. In the language of the later Yogic literature Prāṇāyāma is called Kumbhaka. It is interesting to note here that Patañjali does not use the words Recaka (Exhalation), Kumbhaka (Pause) and Pūraka (Inhalation) anywhere in his Sūtras, although he does refer to these actions. His oldest commentator Vyāsa, who lived in the first century, A.D., also does not use the terms Recaka, Kumbhaka in Pūraka. This circumstance clearly shows that this nomenclature was introduced at a later date. Tracing the history of the development, of not only these terms but many others used in the Yoga Śāstra, would be a fruitful research problem for a student of Yogic literature.

been often interpreted to mean a *subtle psychic force* or a *subtle cosmic element.* We do not think that the original Sanskrit text of Bhagavān Patañjali's *Yoga Sūtras* any way warrants this interpretation. In these Sūtras the word Prāṇa occurs by itself only once[2] and the wording of the Sūtra is so clear that by no stretch of imagination can the word Prāṇa there be taken to refer to anything except breath. In addition to this the word Prāṇa occurs

---

2. प्रच्छर्दनविधारणाभ्यां वा प्राणस्य । P. Y. S., I 34

   Bhagavān Patañjali is discussing the different means of bringing the mind under control. He has suggested various measures and one of them is contained in this Sūtra. The word Pracchardana would always mean *expulsion* and must in this Sūtra refer to breath and not to any subtle psychic force or cosmic element. Vidhāraṇa means retention. When all the three words Pracchardana, Vidhāsaṇa and Prāṇa are taken together, they irresistibly drive us to the conclusion that the word Prāṇa here refers to breath and breath alone. The Sūtras means that an alternative measure for controlling the mind, is available in the alternate expulsion and retention of breath. This is not the place for discussing as to whether this Sūtra कौष्ठयो वायु refers to a particular type of Prāṇāyāma or to Prāṇāyāma in general. Vyās and other commentators have explained Prāṇa occurring in this Sūtra as meaning *air from the chest* and thus have left no ambiguity in the interpretation of the word.

twice in the Sūtras[3] every time being compounded with the word Āyāma. Here again the wording of the original author, Patañjali, is very clear. He positively refers to respiratory movements. The most important commentators of Patañjali's Sūtras have invariably explained Prāṇa to mean breath, in their commentaries on the three Sūtras referred to above.

We definitely know that author of Haṭha texts very often use the word Prāṇa to indicate a subtle psychic Force. But this they do when they talk of the force awakened by the proces of Prāṇāyāma and not of Prāṇāyāma itself.

Even with these authors of Haṭha, the word Prāṇa as it occurs in the compound Prāṇāyāma has only one meaning and it is breath. So our conclusion is that in Yogic literature Prāṇāyāma means only a pause in the movement of breath.

---

3. यमनियमासनप्राणायामप्रत्याहारधारणाध्यानसमाधयोऽष्टावङ्गानि ।
P. Y. S. II 29.

This is the first of the two Sūtras. It lays down the eight successive items of the Yogic curriculum, having Prāṇāyāma as the fourth in order. Then follows the second Sūtra to define the word Prāṇāyāma. तस्मिन्सति श्वासप्रश्वासयोर्गतिविच्छेदः प्राणायामः । P. Y. S. II 49. Here the words Śvāsa and Praśvāsa which can never mean anything else than the air flowing in and flowing out, make the meaning absolutely clear. गतिविच्छेदः *is a pause in the movement.* Thus we see that the word Prāṇa occurring in the technical word Prāṇāyāma, according to Patañjali and his commentators, means breath alone. It never indicates any psychic force or cosmic element.

Patañjali's Four Types of Prāṇāyāma

Bhagavān Patañjali notices four types of Prāṇāyāma, the distinction being based upon the nature of the pause. For instance when the pause is made after a thorough exhalation, that would constitute the first type of Prāṇāyāma. The second type of Prāṇāyāma would be available when the pause comes after a deep inhalation. In both these cases the Yogic student is required to make a special effort for holding his breath either out or in. But in the third and fourth types of Prāṇāyāma the student is not required to make any special effort for holding his breath. The respiratory movement may stop all at once, when the student wants it to stop, the pause being continued over a considerable time without any physical effort on the part of the student. This constitutes the third type of Prāṇāyāma. The fourth type is similar to the third. The only difference between the third and the fourth types, is that in the third the pause comes all at once, whereas in the fourth a similar pause is brought about by many inhalations and exhalations preceding it. The absence of effort in maintaining the pause is common to both the third and the fourth types of Prāṇāyāma.[4]

In the language of the later Yogic literature, the first type of Prāṇāyāma is called *Bāhya*[5] *Kumbhaka,* the second type *Ābhyantara*[5] *Kumbhaka,* and the third and the fourth types are called *Kevala*[6] *Kumbhakas.*

---

4. In stating this fourfold distinction of Prāṇāyāma according to Patañjali, we have followed his commentators. We ourselves have a different interpretation for the Sūtras, concerned.
5. The words Bāhya and Ābhyantara alone are used by Patañjali.

Svātmārāma's Eight Varieties of Prāṇāyāma

Svātmārāma's Sūri, the author of Haṭha-Pradīpikā, the most authoritative text book of Haṭha Yoga, mentions eight[7] varieties of Kumbhaka which is with him another name for Prāṇāyāma. It is interesting to note that the principle of division followed by Svātmārāma in distinguishing his Kumbhakas, is different from the principle adopted by Patañjali. We have seen that Bhagvān Patañjali distinguished the different Prāṇāyāmas, according to the nature of Kumbhaka itself. But Svātmārāma's Sūri tries to make a distinction between a Kumbhaka and a Kumbhaka, not because the nature of the Kumbhakas themselves is different, but because the nature of the inhalation and exhalation between which these Kumbhakas occur, is different. Thus the technique of all the eight Kumbhakas is the same. But the technique of the inhalations

---

6. Some idea of Kevala Kumbhaka can be had from what is known on modern physiology *apnea,* provided it is prolonged. Apnea is defined as a transient cessation of respiration after forcible respiration.

NOTE -- Hereby we do not at all want to suggest that Kevala Kumbhaka is only a prolonged apnea. Although we know what Kevela Kumbhaka is in practice, we have not yet tried any experiments with it for understanding its physiology. And having pledged ourselves to a strictly scientific policy, we cannot make any statement that is not backed up by laboratory evidence. The physiological apnea has been stated here only to convey an idea as to what a Kevala Kumbhaka is like.

7. सूर्यभेदन, उज्जायी, सीत्कारी, शीतली, भस्त्रिका, भ्रामरी, मूर्च्छा and प्लाविनी are the eight varieties of Kumbhaka. We shall first take Ujjāyī and Bhastrikā and then the remaining six varieties.

and exhalations differ in every case. These differences we shall notice when we proceed to study the various Kumbhakas in this handbook.

Different Units for measuring Prāṇāyāma and the relative measures of its Component Parts

Each round of Prāṇāyāma is generally[8] a complex act and consists of *Pūraka* (Inhalation), Kumbhaka (Pause) and Recaka (Exhalation). We want to see what units are prescribed for measuring these parts and what relative measures we should maintain among these component parts of a complex Prāṇāyāma. But before we do so we wish to touch one more point in brief.

It has already been noticed in one of the foregoing foot-notes that neither Patañjali nor Vyāsa uses the words Pūraka, Recaka and Kumbhaka. So we should try here to see what terminology they used instead.

It has already been made clear that Prāṇāyāma is the technical word for Kumbhaka, both with Patañjali as well as Vyāsa. Patañjali also uses the word Vidhāraṇa[9] for Kumbhaka. Pracchardana which occurs in the same Sūtra as Vidhāraṇa is clearly Patanjali's word for Recaka. It is explained by Vyāsa as the forcible expulsion of the air from the chest.

Now the question is what word is used by Bhagavān Patañjali for Pūraka. So far as we understand the text of his Sūtras, we are

8. We have used the word *generally* because in Kevala Kumbhaka there is neither Pūraka nor Recaka.

9. प्रच्छर्दनविधारणाभ्यां वा प्राणस्य । P.Y.S.I 34, where Vyāsa explains Vihāraṇa by the word Prāṇāyāma

afraid, we do no come across any word for Pūraka in his work. We know the words Śvāsa and Praśvāsa used by him in his definition of Prāṇāyāma[10]. But we feel sure that Patañjali uses these words for the air flowing into the lungs and the air flowing out of them respectively. Pūraka is a process and not the air being inhaled. So we want a word in antithesis to Pracchardana or Recaka, which would denote the process. That word we do not find in the text of the Sūtras.[11] We should not understand to mean that Patañjali does not recognize the Pūraka action. That action he does recognize when he refers to Ābhayantara Prāṇāyāma which must be preceded after Pūraka. Our contention is that in

---

10. Vide foot-note 2, Chap III.

11. We know the extreme elasticity of the rules of interpretaion of Sanskrit texts. We are sure that a Pandita versed in large and rhetories will successfully prove that Śvāsa occurring in the Sūtra तस्मिन्सति श्वासप्रश्वासयोर्गतिविच्छेदः प्राणायामः । means Pūraka. But we are not sure whether we will be able to explain *consistently* all the Sūtras of Patañjali bearing on Prāṇāyāma, from a *practical points of view,* and yet will interpret Śvāsa as the process of Pūraka.

    The question we are discussing here is very complicated. It is rendered more complicated by the successive commentators who were anxious to find up-to-date information in the Sūtras of Patañjali. Our attitude is to make the Sūtras consistent in themselves, irrespective of the later developments of Yogic exercises and Yogic terminology. We do not think that Patañjali's would be condemned as a writer of an incomplete Yogic text, simply because he does not refer expressly to the different types of Prāṇāyāma described by later writers on Yoga.

the text of the Sūtras itself, there is no word explicitly denoting the process of Pūraka.

So we find that Patañjali's word for Kumbhaka is either Prāṇāyāma or Vidhāraṇa and for Recaka his word is Pracchardana. Patañjali does not use any word for the process of Pūraka.

Next we go to the units laid down for measuring Kumbhaka, Recaka and Pūraka. The Yogins of old were very particular about the mathematical accuracy of their processes. They were anxious to measure everything precisely in terms of time-units and space-units. We must remember that these seers had neither clocks nor any other instruments that would measure accurately very small fractions of time. So they had to depend upon time units determined by some physical action. Each time-unit was called Mātrā. The following physical actions were singled out to denote a time-unit or Mātrā :-

(i) The Twinkling of an Eye.

(ii) Time taken to pronounce a short vowel.

(iii) Time necessary for touching one's knee thrice followed by a clap.

(iv) Time occupied by one normal respiration.

(V) Time taken up in pronouncing the sacred syllable ॐ etc. etc.

Our readers will immediately see that this sort of calculation is very vague. Nor do the units agree mutually. Not that the ancient seers were unmindful of this fact. The very attempt to introduce *different* standards for determining the time-unit, shows that none of them was found to be quite satisfactory. But it has to be remembered that the practice of Prāṇāyāma was taught by the master to his pupil in person. So whatever the length of the time-unit accepted by a particular school of Yogins, the student could learn to note it accurately from his master. Moreover at the time of practising Prāṇāyāma, one has after all to *judge* the *Mātrā,* that is, had to determine it by a mental process. So there was no difficulty in teaching accurately the length of time that constituted a Mātrā; of course in each case as much accuracy would be ensured as was available by *judging* the time. Today a practical student of Yoga need not worry himself over the diversity of these time-units. He should cultivate the habit of counting one, two, three.... at the interval of a second. A few minutes' practice in consultation with his watch, will make him perfect. Those that so wish it, should prefix ॐ to each number. ॐ one, ॐ two, ॐ three and so on.

Next we come to space-unit. This was necessary for measuring the force with which he inhalations and exhalations were practised. In a forced exhalation the current of the expired air can be felt upto a particular distance from the end of the nose. The more forcible the exhalation, the greater will be the space across which the flow can be detected. Very light organic fibres were suggested to be used for detecting this current. The affected space was measured in fingers, etc. So the length of the air current determined the degree of pressure with which one was exhaling in Recaka.

The way of determining the strength of Pūraka as described by the commentators of the original Sūtras, is somewhat difficult to understand. The measure of the strength of Pūraka must naturally lie along the inward flow of the inspired air. In our humble opinion the sensations which have been described as making the space-unit to Pūraka are extremely vague and may not give even a tolerably accurate idea even to an advanced student of Yoga. So we do not attempt any description of this space-unit here.

For all practical purposes, spiritual as well as physical, the following hints will suffice : -

(i) The length of time to be given to Pūraka should be half of what is being given to Recaka.[12]

(ii) Throughout Pūraka, the inhalation should be uniform.[13] That is the strength of the flow should be of the same degree throughout. The act should neither be slowed down or hurried up.

(iii) Every Pūraka must end quietly. Many people are in the habit of contracting most violently muscles of the whole body at this stage. It is to be noted that no amount of violence done to muscles other than respiratory, will enable a person to draw in even one additional ml. of air.

The time-unit is applicable even to Kumbhaka. The practical method of measuring the length of time occupied by Pūraka, and Recaka that we have described above, should also be used for Kumbhaka.

---

12. We shall state later on what time should be given to Recaka.

13. Either in the case of Pūraka or in the case of Recaka if the time-unit is taken care of, and a uniform flow of breath is secured, the space unit takes care of itself.

Having studied the Mātrā by which we can measure Pūraka, Kumbhaka and Recaka independent of one another, we now proceed to see what relation these three component parts of Prāṇāyāma should bear among themselves so far as their duration is concerned. In this connection the most favoured view is to have the durations of Pūraka, Kumbhaka and Recaka in the proportion of 1:4:2. According to another tradition, this proportion should be 1:2:2. Thus if Pūraka consists of sixteen Mātrās, Kumbhaka should be of sixty-four and recaka of thirty-two Mātrās, according to the first proportion. And according to the second proportion for sixteen Mātrās of Pūraka, both Kumbhaka and Recaka should have thirty-two each. There is a third tradition which lays down the same measure for all the three parts of Prāṇāyāma.

This is all right so far as the *relative* durations of Pūraka, Kumbhaka and Recaka are concerned. But what should be the absolute duration of Pūraka or Kumbhaka or Recaka, one of which being fixed, would fix up the other two. Here the safest course would be first to settle the Mātrās of Kumbhaka and then to follow any of the proportions stated in the foregoing paragraph. Individually we are in favour of the second proportion for a beginner, although an advanced student can follow the first proportion without any danger to himself. Again in fixing up the Mātrās of Kumbhaka, a beginner should see that he can hold his breath very comfortably during the whole duration. Not only this but he should also see that he is able to perform Recaka in due proportion with an equal degree of comfort. The whole practice of Prāṇāyāma should be gone through with utmost ease and comfort. No jerks, no violence, no undue sense of suffocation should be there at any stage of Prāṇāyāma.

We very strongly advise the *beginners to start only with Pūraka and Recaka, the respective durations being in the proportion of 1:2. The physical culturist can get all the advantages he wants to derive from Prāṇāyāma, by the practice of Pūraka and Recaka only. Even a spiritual culturist can make a good deal of progress without the practice of Kumbhaka. So there should be absolutely no hurry about taking to Kumbhaka. So also when Kumbhaka is started, it should be very slowly and cautiously developed. Kumbhaka is the one thing in Prāṇāyāma which demands the utmost attention on the part of a student of Yoga. If, however, it is developed with due caution and care, there is nothing dangerous about it or about Prāṇāyāma as a whole.*

The duration in Prāṇāyāma should be judged mentally. Both the physical culturists and the spiritual culturists should practice Prāṇāyāma with utmost concentration. The mind should very closely follow the movement of breath. In numbering the Mātrās the concentration of the breath is disturbed. Again the spirit culturist, as he advances, is required to concentrate on different points either inside the body or outside it. In this work the numbering of the Matras causes a little distraction. Those that can manage the numbering business without allowing their concentration being affected, may take it if they so choose.

In a discussion of Prāṇāyāma a reference to Nāḍīs is absolutely necessary. Hence we proceed to a consideration of these.

The Nāḍīs

In later Yogic literature the Nāḍīs play a very important part. But either in Bhagavān Patañjali or in the oldest commentary on his Sūtras written by Vyāsa, the word Nāḍīs occurs only once.[14] There again the reference is to a Nāḍī that is comparatively of small importance. The total number of Nāḍīs present in the human body has been variously estimated. According to one author it is 72,000, where as according to another it is as huge as 350,000. Nāḍīs are, however, distinguished as those of comparatively small importance, those of some importance and those of great importance. One is singled out as the most important of the whole lot. The number of Nāḍīs of some importance is stated to be either ten or fourteen. There is however, perfect agreement among the authors of Yogic literature in mentioning the number of the more important Nāḍīs as three[15] and that of the most important as one.[16]

Can we identify these Nāḍīs with any of the anatomical structures known to modern science ? Upto now various attempts[17]

---

14. It is in the Sūtra कूर्मनाड्यां स्थैर्यम् P.Y.S.III 31.
15. इडा, पिङ्गला and सुषुम्ना.
16. सुषुम्ना.
17. By far boldest attempt in this direction has been made by Dr. V.G. Rele of Bombay in his book. *The Mysterious Kuṇḍalinī.* The books is certainly thought-provoking and Dr. Rele has worked hard at his thesis. He has taken full advantage of his knowledge of modern anatomy and physiology, and some of his guess-work has every chance of standing the laboratory tests. He has explored a very large field of Yogic physiology and anatomy, and every student of Yoga will ever feel indebted to him for his labour of love. We heartily recommend the book to our readers' attention. But after all his conclusions are based upon *mere speculation.* Dr. Rele has not tried a single experiment in the laboratory, nor has he taken much care to consult the practical experience of the students of

have been made for such an identification, at least in the cases of the important Nāḍis but all of them, so far we know, have been of a literary character. No strictly scientific effort has been made to this day. Being pledged to a policy of strict scientific accuracy, we cannot accept the results of the efforts as scientifically sound. We too have many hypothetical conclusions regarding Yogic anatomy and physiology. But we do not wish to place them before the public as scientific, unless we test them in the laboratory.

Yoga. As such, we are afraid, we cannot accept his conclusions as scientifically sound. Nay, we have serious doubts regarding the accuracy of many of his interpretations, and the whole book seems to be of doubtful scientific value. Dr. Rele very frankly admits in his preface to the book that his interpretations are 'possible suggestions only'. Another attempt in this direction that deserves special mention here, is that of the great Swāmī Vivekānanda. His lectures on Rāja - Yoga are full of interpretations of Yogic things in the light of modern sciences. We are sorry to note here that the Swāmījī's attempt suffers from the same drawbacks as the work of Dr. Rele. The whole structure is based upon the treacherous sands of speculation. Being pledged to accept nothing, in the field of scientific interpretation, as sound, unless it is backed up by laboratory evidence, we cannot accept the conclusions of the great master as scientific. We do not want to be misunderstood. We make a distinction between Yoga as a reliable guide for spiritual evolution, and Yoga being scientifically interpreted. Since time immemorial, Yoga is being practised as a means to self-realization. The traditional practices are as sound as anything known to modern science. We have adamantine faith in the efficacy of these exercises as a means to spiritual evolution. But the

For the information of our readers, however, we shall mention the modern interpretations put upon the words Nāḍī, Suṣumnā, Iḍā and Piñgalā. Without going into details, we shall also broadly

---

scientific interpretations of the Yogic practices and Yogic anatomy and physiology, is quite a different thing. It means trying experiments upon these practices in the laboratory according to the strict scientific methods and basing one's conclusions on the results thus obtained. Evidently Swāmī Vivekānanda never tried these experiments and had to resort to speculation. This is a statement of facts and there is no intention to find fault with the Swāmījī's. His lectures on Rāja-Yoga are master-pieces of inspirational literature. We ourselves owe a deep debt of gratitude to the great master, especially as the author of his *Lectures in Rāja- Yoga.* A third attempt which compels attention is that of Dr. Brajendra Nath Seal. In his very valuable book, The Positive Sciences of the Ancient Hindus, the Doctor attempts scientific interpretations of some of the yogic anatomical terms. Even though his interpretations are better than those of Swāmī Vivekānanda and anticipate in particular respects those of Dr. Rele, they cannot be treated as scientifically sound. They are not supported by any laboratory evidence. But the oldest attempt in the direction of scientifically interpreting the Yogic anatomy seems to have been made by Major B.D. Basu who published an article on this subject in *The Theosophist* as far back as 1888. His interpretations though speculative certainly claim great admiration. It is a pity that those who followed Major Basu did not take advantage of his precious work. It is greatly suprising to find Dr. Rele not acknowledging his debt both to Major Basu and Dr. Seal, each of whom has anticipated some of his interpretations. Perhaps he did not know their works.

say whether these interpretations are acceptable to us or not. Our acceptance or otherwise has, however, absolutely no scientific value, as it is based upon mere guesswork today.[18]

Nāḍīs have been identified with the nerves of modern anatomy. Although there are places in Yoga literature where the word Nāḍīs has definitely been used in some other sense, this interpretation is on the whole acceptable to us. In fact the description [19] of the Nāḍīs in general given in one of the Yogic text-books, is so vivid and accurate, that there is little scope for any difference of opinion regarding the interpretation.

---

18. We are trying our best to equip our laboratory with such apparatus as would enable us to conduct experiments on the Nāḍīs. Everything else is ready. And by the grace of the Lord, we feel sure we shall soon have the desired equipment also. We are glad to state that our Labratory equipment has greatly improved since the preceding statement was made and our experimental work is going on apace.
19. नाड्यस्तु ता अधोवक्त्राः पद्मतन्तुनिभाः स्थिताः ।
    पृष्ठवंश समाश्रित्य... .... ।। Śiva-Saṁhitā II 17
    (These Nāḍīs are like the fibres of a lotus, and being supported by the vertebral column, spread downwards.)

The same may be said about Suṣumnā. It is explained as the spinal cord. We do not *much*[20] object to this interpretation.

Idā and Piñgala are identified by Swāmī Viveknānda[21] with the sensory and motor tracts of the spinal cord. We cannot accept this interpretation, however, as it does not tally with the description of these Nāḍīs in the original Sanskrit texts. Dr. Rele's interpretation[22] of Idā and piñgala as the mere chains of central ganglia, one on either side of the middle line of the vertebral column, is almost acceptable to us. In fact hypothetically we had come almost to this very conclusion even before Dr. Rele's book was published. Even now, however, we have some difficulties in

---

20. We say *much* because we too think that Suṣumnā is to be identified with the spinal cord. But we are not sure as to whether it is to be identified with the entire cord or only with a part of it, that is, the spinal canal. However we are more inclined to identify Suṣumnā with the spinal canal. The whole trouble about exact anatomical interpretation of Suṣumnā is due to its identification with Brahmanāḍī at several places in ancient Sanskrit literature. However so far as Sanskrit texts on Haṭhayoga are concerned Suṣumnā mean Spinal Canal alone.

21. "Thus asserts the Swāmījī in his *Lecture on Rāja Yoga :-*
The columns of sensory and motor fibres in the spinal cord are the Iḍā and Piñgalā of the Yogins. They are the main channcels through which the afferent and efferent currents travel."

22. Dr. Rele in his Mysterious Kuṇḍalinī writes :-
"From the description of the Nāḍīs. Iḍā and Piñgalā, they are nothing but the gangliated cords of the sympathetic system. Which we know are situated (one?) on each side of the spinal column". p.35.

fully accepting this identification of Idā and Piñgalā as even hypothetically final. Most probably we will have to modify it a little.

We have thus far studied the speculative identification of the Nāḍīs. Now we go to note a few more points concerning the, because they often occur in Yogic literature. In fact in our Laboratory our colleague Dr. S.L. Vinekar has succeeded in scientifically studying the discharges from the mucous membrane of the two nostrils and found that the discharges from the two nostrils give different electric potentials. This study may help us later on to decide the truth or otherwise of this belief with the help of more sensitive pieces of apparatus.

It is believed that inhalation through the right nostril creates heat in the body and inhalation through the left nostril creates cold. This has most probably led Yogins to describe the right Nāḍī, that is, Piñgalā as Sūrya-Nāḍī. Sūrya means the sun and is the symbol of heat. In the same way Iḍā is called Nāḍī, Candra, the *moon,* standing as a symbol of cold.

Again the word Nāḍīs stands for the nostrils. Thus Sūrya-Nāḍī means either Piñgalā or the right nostril, and Candra Nāḍī means either Iḍā or the left nostril.

What has been said upto now is intended to get the modern student of Yoga in touch with the traditional phrascology. We have also given some hints to the practical student of Yoga. Before closing this chapter, we shall, however, make some more practical suggestions to our readers.

Oxygen Value versus Nerve Culture Value of Prāṇāyāma

The Westerner looks to exercise in deep breathing mainly from the point of view of its oxygen value.[23] He appreciates these exercises principally because they give him a larger quantity of oxygen to vitalize his system. With us the oxygen value of Prāṇāyāma is subordinate. We prize it more for its usefullness in nerve culture.[24] We make this statement not only for the spiritual culturist but for the physical culturist also. Let it be, however, borne in mind that even the oxygen value is not below our attention.

The Place

Hence whether the student takes to Yoga for spiritual culture or physical, he must practise Prāṇāyāma in a very well ventilated place. He should not allow himself, however, to be exposed to a strong draught. Practising Prāṇāyāma in the open is extremely healthy. A spiritual culturist should, however, see that he avoids all disturbing factors. In his case the need for utmost concentration is extreme. Hence, it is desirable that he chooses a thoroughly ventilated room which is free from mosquitoes etc. and where he

---

23. We are conducting a number of experiments in our laboratory on the oxygen value of Prāṇāyāma. The whole material will be placed before the public when it is ready for publication. The data being collected are likely to add to our present day knowledge of metabolism.
24. For a full discussion on this very intersting but controversial point, we refer our readers to Yoga-Mīṃāṃsā. In that journal we have put forth convincing evidence based on laboratory and clinical experimentation.

would be left to himself. Even the possibility of being disturbed, comes in the way of perfect concentration. If he could reserve a room for this work and build up a spiritual atmosphere there, it will help him a good deal in his work.

The seat

For a spiritual culturist the traditional arrangement of seating is excellent. A carpet of Kuśa[25] grass, with a well tanned deer hide,[26] spread on it, the hide in its turn being covered with a daily washed piece of thick khaddar, makes a very comfortable seat. The pleasures of such a seat are the peculiar privilege of those god-intoxicated aspiring souls who seek salvation through Yoga. The thrilling spiritual experiences that this seat affords to the student from day to day, make it more attractive to him than even the throne of an emperor !

A physical culturist is by no means barred from using such a seat. Even to him it will have its own attraction. But he need not be very particular about its use. He can practise his Prāṇāyāma

---

25. In the absence of a Kuśa grass carpet, any other grass carpet will serve the purpose.
26. Those that may have a conscientious objection to the use of a hide should make use of a thick woollen cloth folded over several times

while sitting, or while standing or even while walking.[27] It is with the intention of giving the physical culturist an opportunity to practise Prāṇāyāma even in walking,[28] and yet not to go against the traditional rules of Prāṇāyāma, that we have arranged to give in this part of the present handbook, the technique of Ujjāyī. This is the only type of Prāṇāyāma allowed by the Yoga Sāśtra to be practised even while one walks. It is principally for this reason that we teach Ujjāyī to every man that comes to us for a Yogic instruction, be it for his body or for his mind.

The Posture

If the physical culturist prefers to practise Prāṇāyāma while walking, no question of posture arises with him. Again if he chooses to have the practise of Prāṇāyāma in a standing position, the question of Āsana is of no consequence to him. He should,

---

27. We cannot much appreciate the advice given to their follwers by paticular physical culturist, to practise Prāṇāyāma while taking violent muscular exrecise. So far as we understand the physiological aspects of both Prāṇāyāma and violent muscular work, we have no hesitation in saying that it is impossible to practise Prāṇāyāma while violent muscular work is being done. One may hold his breath for a time during such a work and give it the dignified name of Prāṇāyāma or Kumbhaka but any attempt to claim Prāṇāyāmic advantage for such a holoding of breath, is as unscientific as it is misleading.

28. गच्छता तिष्ठता कार्यम् । उज्जाय्याख्यं तु कुंभकम् ।। Haṭha Pradīpikā, 1152 (The Ujjāyī Prāṇāyāma may be practised even while standing or while walking.)

however, stand erect and rest his hands on his ilaic bones.[29] (*Vide* Fig. 24). So also if a physical culturist thinks of going through the Prāṇāyāmic exercises while sitting, he should assume as erect posture[30] and rest his hands on his knees. It is not necessary for him to assume any of the Yogic postures. The spiritual culturist shall always sit in one of the meditative poses described in the last chapter. The importance of Āsana in the process of his evolution, can never be exaggerated. The principal meditative poses are Siddha, Padma, Svanstika and Sama. Of these we should specially recommend to our reader the first and the third. Both these Āsana have a special spiritual value.

FIG. 24. - Correct standing Position for Ujjāyī.

---

29. For a full discussion on the physiological significance of the technique of Prāṇāyāma we strongly recommend our articles in *Yoga-Mīmāṃsā* to our readers. However, a few points have been made clear in this handbook in the foot-notes. It may be said that every point in the technique has its own scientific importance and should be carefully attended to.

30. Our article on the meditative poses appearing in Yoga-Mīmāsā, Vol. III, explains the hygienic value of an erect posture. The article is intended for the physical culturist as well as the spiritual culturist. However, those students who want more scientificallt studies values of postures are referred to pages 34 to 49 of Yogic Therapy written conjointly by the present author, and Dr. S.L.Vinekar and published by the Central Health Ministry, New Delhi.

Mudrā

Spiritual culturists will do well to note in short the technique of what is known as Jñāna-Mudrā, the *symbol of Knowledge.* This Mudrā is practised as an accompaniment of a meditative pose. The palms are fully stretched out and the tip of the index finger, that is, finger next to the thumb, is made to touch the tip of the thumb of the same hand. In this action, it is the forefinger that is bent to meet the thumb, the latter advancing a little, no doubt, to meet its fellow. Fig. 25 illustrates this Jñāna-Mudrā by itself, whereas Figs. 21 and 23 illustrate the same when practised as a part of Svastikāsana and Samāsana respectively.

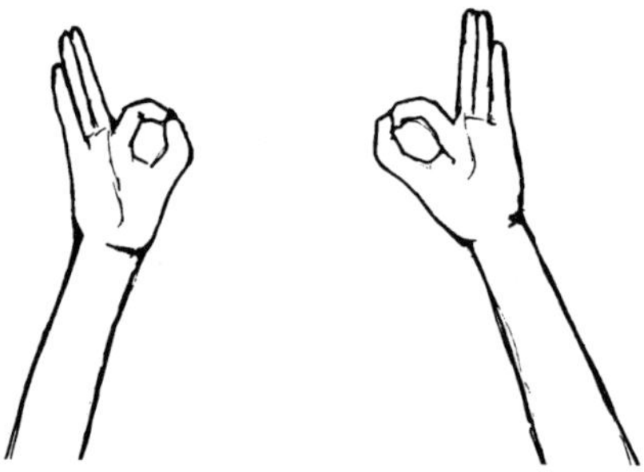

FIG. 25. - Jñānamudra or the Symbol of Knowledge.

Bandha

The different Bandhas, namely, Uḍḍiāna, Jālandhra and Mūla, that play a prominent part in the practice of Prāṇāyāma have already been described in the last chapter. Under no circumstances should Kumbhaka be practised without Jālandhra Bandha. The practice of the other two Bandhas is optional.[31]

31. The practice of Kumbhaka with the simultaneous exercise of all the three Bandhas is *highly dangerous,* if done without proper care and caution. No student of Yoga should indulge in this exercise without the help of an expert.

Time

For a physical culturist any time half an hour before the meal, of four hours and a half after a full meal is available. Light refreshment does not preclude the practice of Prāṇāyāma after some two hours.

A spiritual culturist should practise Prāṇāyāma twice a day, that is, morning and evening to begin with. As he advances he may take advantages of the midday and ultimately of midinight. Every time he must see that he has a thoroughly light stomach before he starts his Prāṇāyāma. His meals must always be moderate. One meal plan is the best for him. He must allow some six hours between his last meal and his exercises. Even after taking a moderate quantity of milk, he must not take to his practice at least for two hours.

In the morning the exercise of Prāṇāyāma should be tried after the cleansing processes of Dhauti, Basti etc., and even after the Āsanas. In the evening Prāṇāyāma should come after the Āsanas.[32] If any meditation is being practised, Prāṇāyāma should precede it.

The conclusion

In concluding this short chapter on Prāṇāyāma, we have to point out to our reader that the subject is very vast and requires volumes of information for its full treatment. These notes are intended for enabling the reader to follow the technique of the

32. Here we have simply indicated the sequence of the different Yogic practices. We do not mean that the other practices must necessarily be gone through before one takes to Prāṇāyāma.

different types of Prāṇāyāma intelligently, and also to help him in his Yogic practices. Prāṇāyāma is by far the most useful exercise for a physical culturist. To the spiritual culturist its importance is supreme. We are trying our best to supply scientific information to both these classes of readers in the volumes of Yoga-Mīṃāṃsā

We earnestly request our readers never to allow their enthusiasm to get the better of reason. Prāṇāyāma is a weapon that easily lends itself to abuse. In playing with Prāṇāyāma, a man plays with his nerves, heart and lungs. Undue strain or imperfect methods in Prāṇāyāma may damage these parts permanently. So every one should proceed into this practice with due caution and care. When this is done and when our instructions are attentively and faithfully followed, Prāṇāyāma is perfectly safe. When rightly done, Prāṇāyāma will never fail to ensure supreme vitality for the body and eternal peace for the mind.

CHAPTER IV

UJJĀYI

The Name

In the last chapter we have explained the meaning of the world Prāṇāyāma. It has also been stated that the author of *Haṭha-Pradīpikā* gives eight varieties of Prāṇāyāma, one of which is Ujjāyī. We do not definitely know why this particular type of Prāṇāyāma is called Ujjāyī. We may, however, venture two conjectures about this name. In ancient India greetings consisted of the word Jaya which was always loudly pronounced. Hence the word Jaya and the cognate words cannot be closely associated with loud pronunciation. Now the chief characteristic of the Ujjāyī Prāṇāyāma is the loud noise produced, as well be seen in the technique, by a partial closure of the glottis. Hence it is possible that this Prāṇāyāma is called Ujjāyī to distinguish it from other varieties. Our conjecture is rendered *probable,* when we take into consideration the two following facts (1) the prefix Ud occurring in the name Ujjāyī (). means, aloud. (2) Ujjāpī, a variant reading noticed by Bramānanda, in his commentary on *Haṭha-Pradīpīkā,* actually means *pronounced loudly*. Most probably the variant Ujjāpī was suggested because the original word Ujjāyī was not so clear in its meaning. So in all probability Ujjāyī also means *pronounced loudly*.

There is some possibility of the Prāṇāyāma being called Ujjāyī because its practice was supposed to lead one to success. Ujjāyī might be interpreted to mean *leading* to success.

The Technique[1]

The general instructions regarding the time, the place, the seat, the posture etc., given in the last chapter, are all applicable to Ujjāyī. We shall now give the particular technique of this Prāṇāyāma.

Pūraka

Before we describe the technique of Pūraka in Ujjāyī, we wish to refer to a point in the technique of Prāṇāyāma in general, so far as the inhalation and exhalation are concerned.

Generally speaking, during the course of Prāṇāyāma one is required to keep closed one nostril or the other, and in Kumbhaka both the nostrils. What is the orthodox way of closing the nostrils in Yoga ? Tradition requires this work to be done in a particular manner. According to our view this manner of closing the nostrils is not very comfortable but it is also scientific. The right palm is spread out. The index and the middle fingers are turned down, the other two fingers and thumb remain extended. (*Vide* Fig. 26). Now the thumb and the extended fingers are placed on the bridge of the nose, the thumb on the right side of it, and the fingers on the left. Then, if the right nostril is to be closed, the fingers are allowed

---

1. Our readers are requested to master the chapter on respiration before trying to practise Ujjāyī according to the technique given here. The technique given here is intended for enabling the reader to pick up the practice. Nearly every point in the technique has a scientific explanation in its support. Some of these explanations are attempted in the foot-notes. For detailed discussion the readers are referred to *Yoga-Mīṃāṃsā.*

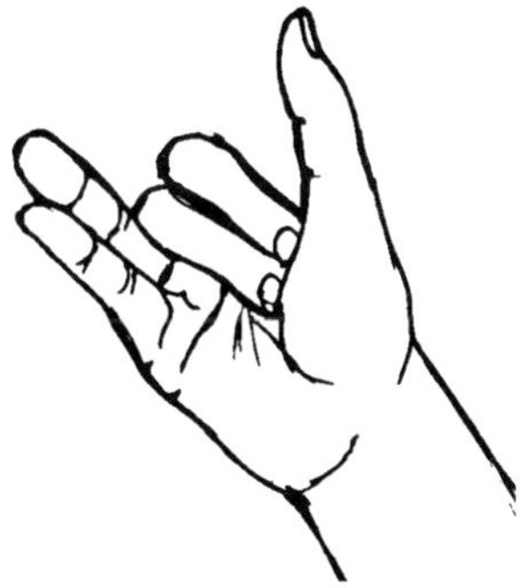

FIG. 26. - Preparation for Closing of the Nostrils.

to retain their position but the thumb is slided downwards, and made to sit tight upon the elastic right nostril, pressing it against the septum at the side and the hand bone above. (*Vide* Fig. 28). Again, if the left nostril is to be closed, the thumb is taken back to its original position on the bridge of the nose and the fingers are slided down to sit tightly upon the let nostril, pressing the elastic part against the septum at the side and the nasal bone above. (*Vide* Fig. 29). If both the nostrils are to be closed, both the thumb and the fingers are slided down, pressing against the nostrils as in

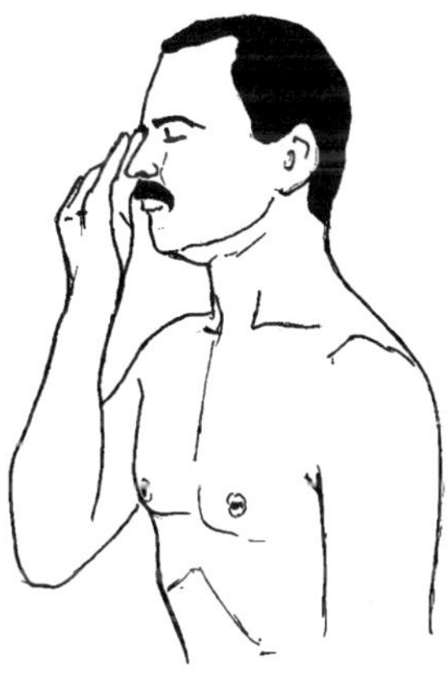

FIG. 28. - The Right Nostril Closed.

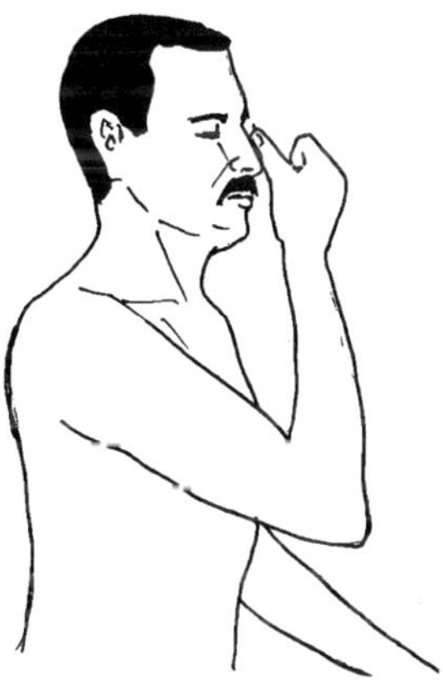

FIG. 29. - The Left Nostril Closed.

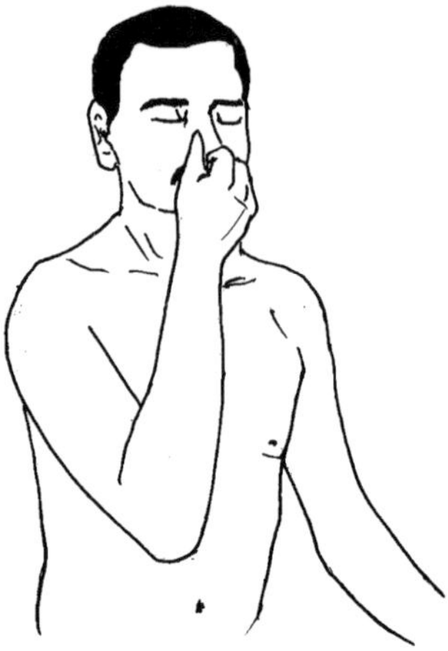

FIG. 30. - Both the Nostrils Closed

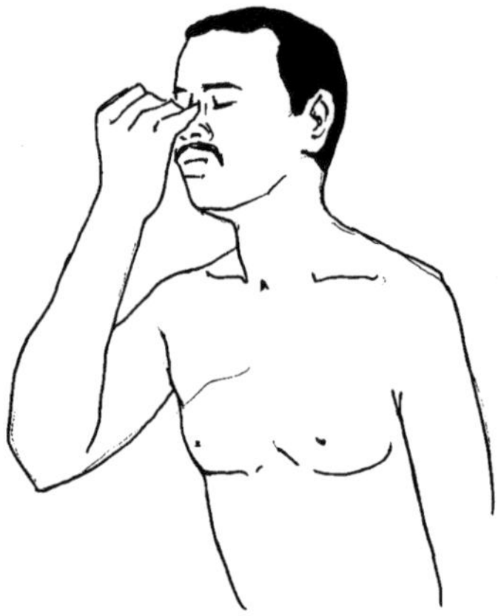

FIG. 31. - Both the Nostrils Open

the last two cases. (*Vide* Fig. 30). But if both the nostrils are to be kept open, there are two Positions for the right hand. The fingers and the thumb may rest on the bridge of the nose or the right hand may be taken down to rest on the knees shown in Fig. 21 or 23. The first position (*Vide* Fig. 31) is preferable, when alternating with the open nostrils, one of the nostrils is to be kept closed, as in the case of Ujjāyī. But the second position should be preferred, if there is no alternate closure of the nostrils. Now we come to Pūraka.

Every Pūraka, including the first, is to start complete exhalation. In Ujjāyī, breath is to be drawn in through both the nostrils, In drawing in the breath the work is to be done with the chest. The student is to expand it and the air will automatically rush in. Throughout the inhalation, the glottis is to be partially closed. This partial closure of the glottis will produce a continuous sound like the sound that is produced in sobbing. The difference is that in sobbing the sound is abrupt and broken. Here it is continuous. At the time of inhalation the facial muscles or the muscles of the nose should not be contracted. The contraction of facial muscles is of absolutely no use in inhalation. Some people are in the habit of having ugly contortions of the whole face, when they try to inhale. (*Vide* Fig. 27). This is to be completely avoided.

Special care is to be taken of the abdominal muscles. They should be kept under proper control with a very slight contraction which is to be maintained throughout the inhalation. Fig. 32 illustrates[2] this control. It can be better observed in Fig. 33 which shows a side view of the position. Fig. 34 represents the controlled abdomen at the end of the inhalation. Here again Fig. 35 which

FIG. 32. - Starting Inhalation with Controlled Abdominal Muscles (*Front View*)

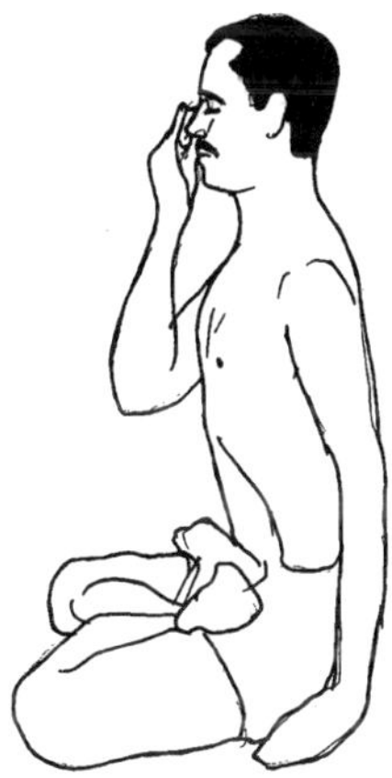

FIG. 33. - Starting Inhalation with Controlled Abdominal Muscles (*Side View*)

2. In this and the following pictures given in this chapter, the position of the right hand on the nose does not refer to Ujjāyī. The photographs are intended to be of general use inillustrating positions in Prāṇāyāma.

FIG. 34. Full Inhalation with Controlled Abdominal Muscles (*Front View*)

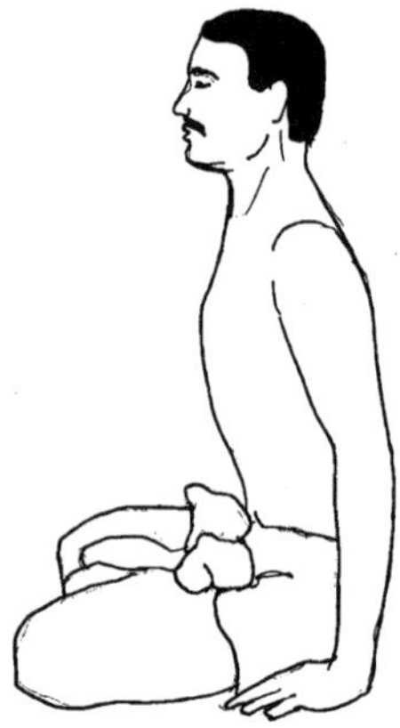

FIG. 35. Full Inhalation with Controlled Abdominal Muscles (*Side View*)

gives a side view of this very position, affords a better idea. The Western physical culturists advise their followers to draw out the abdomen at the time of inhalation. In our opinion this is due to some wrong conceptions about the physiology of deep breathing. They appear to be under the impression that they can admit a large quantity of fresh air and consequently of oxygen, if they were to draw out their abdomen. But in the laboratory evidence that we have collected in the Āśrama, we have found this to be an error of judgment. The fact is that the controlled abdomen allows at a time more oxygen to be inhaled than the protracted abdomen. So far as the culture of the nerves is concerned, controlled abdominal muscles have a decided advantage over protracted abdominal muscles in which condition they are kept relaxed.[3]

3. For full and convincing information on this extremely vital point read our article 'Ujjāyī Prāṇāyāma' Explained in *Yoga-Mīmāṃsā,* Vol IV.

We do not say Prāṇāyāma, but purposely use the word *deep breathing.* As discussed in chapter XIII, the physiological effects of Prāṇāyāma are vastly different from those of deep breathing. It is, therefore, wrong to use the two words as equivalents of each other. To illustrate full inhalation with protracted abdomen, we have given Fig. 36. Fig. 37 represents the side view of the same. A comparison between Figs. 35 and 37 will very vividly indicate the contrast between a controlled and a protracted abdomen.

The whole course of inhalation must be smooth and uniform. The accompanying sound due to the friction offered by the partially closed glottis, should also be of a low but sweet and uniform pitch. All friction in the nose, especially in the olfactory region, should be cautiously avoided. It is this friction that is very often responsible for disorders of the brain at times from the wrong methods of Prāṇāyāma. When the limit of inhalation is reached there should be no convulsive effort at snatching an additional

FIG. 36. Full Inhalation with Protracted Abdomen (*Front View*)

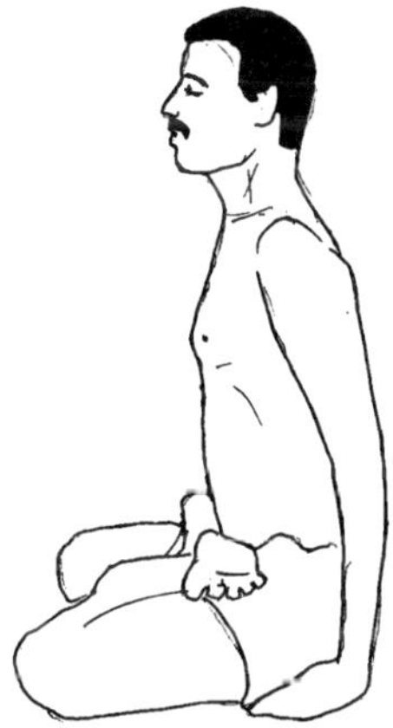

FIG. 37. Full Inhalation with Protracted Abdomen (*Side View*)

breath. No amount of muscle twisting will draw in even one more ml. of air. As soon as the inhalation is completed, Kumbhaka should start.

Kumbhaka

Out of the various types of Kumbhakas referred to in the preceding chapter, Ujjāyī requires Ābhyanatara Kumbhaka, that is, Kumbhaka practised after deep inhalation. The first thing that demands our attention is this Kumbhaka is the complete closure of the glottis. This thoroughly shuts off the passage to and from the lungs. The second thing is the practice of Jālandhara-Bandha (*Vide* pp. 25, 26) and the third is the shutting of the nostrils. The tightly closed glottis establishes the first and the most effective line of defence against the inspired air that constantly tries to break through the air passage during the interval of Kumbhaka. Jālandhara-Bandha by thoroughly contracting the oral pharynx offers the second line of defence. The third line of defence requires no explanation. It is to be noted that when the first line fails, the second and third lines are not able to successfully withstand the onset of the air. Nor is it desirable to attempt such a thing, because such an effort is likely to lead to untoward consequences. The second and third lines are there, only to support the first line in its work.

It is to be borne in mind that the glottis will be able to do its work only so long as the walls of the chest stand firm with the elevated ribs. So the contraction of the muscles of inspiration secured at the end of inhalation, is to be maintained throughout Kumbhaka.

The slight contraction of the abdomen is to be carefully maintained. As will be shown in the last chapter of the present handbook, the real advantages of Kumbhaka lies in this abdominal contraction. Here we must make a brief reference to the popular belief according to which the real advantage of Kumbhaka consists in the larger quantities of oxygen being absorbed into the system, on account of the retention of air in the lungs. We have conducted laboratory experiments to test the truth of this belief: and we have found that there is not much truth in it.[4]

The time limit of Kumbhaka should be made to depend upon two things: (1) While Kumbhaka lasts, no serious sense of suffocation should be experienced. (2) At the end of Kumbhaka, the student must have as much control over his lungs as would make a smooth and proportionate Recaka possible. If these conditions are attended to, there is no danger of damaging either the lungs or the heart, in the case of a man of average health.[5]

The time proportion between Pūraka and Kumbhaka is either 1:4 or 1:2 as stated in the last chapter. A beginner will do well to follow the latter. But whatever the proportion, the measure of Kumbhaka should first be determined as stated in the foregoing paragraph and then a proportionate time be fixed for Pūraka.

When Kumbhaka is to end, first relieve the pressure from the left nostril, then unlock Jālandhara-Bandha and afterwards partially

4. The experiments referring to this point are published in *Yoga-Mīṃāṃsā*, Vol. IV.

5. People suffering from pulmonary or cardiac disorders will do well not to practise Prāṇāyāma, and especially Kumbhaka, save under expert supervision.

open the glottis. The thorax is to be relaxed only when the air passage is left open. With relaxation of the chest Recaka starts.

Recaka

Recaka is be done through the left nostril. At no stage during Recaka should the student lose his control over the lungs. The relaxation of the chest should be slow and uniformly progressive to the end. The glottis should all along remain partially closed. The frictional sound due to this partial closure, should be of a low but uniform pitch.

From the very beginning of Recaka, the abdominal muscles undergo greater and greater contraction. Even when the chest shrinks to its lowest size, the abdomen should continue to contract, till at last the last ml. of the inhaled air is expelled. Figs. 38 and 39 represent a thoroughly contracted abdomen. This does not mean that in Recaka any amount of strain can be put upon the system. It only means that the exhalation should be as thorough as can be secured without involving any undue strain. Our readers may,

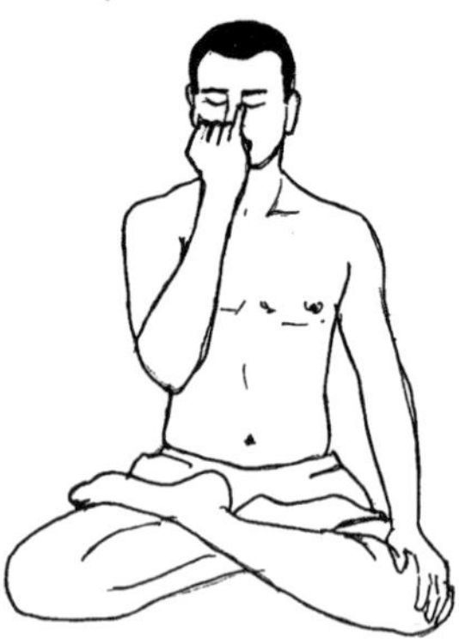

FIG. 38. Full Exhalation *(Front View)*

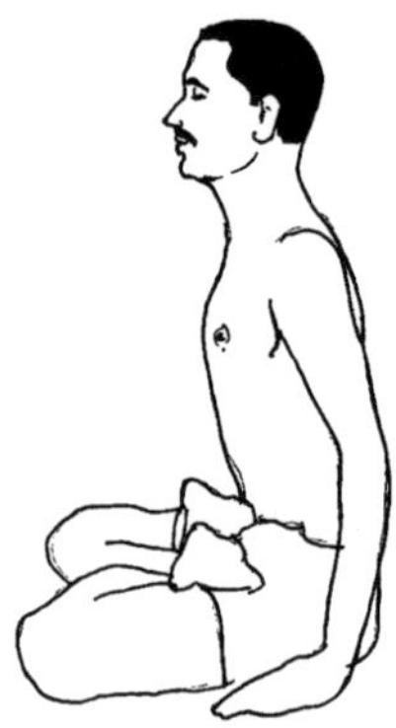

FIG. 39. Full Exhalation *(Side View)*

however, note here that in Recaka there is less possibility of unduly straining oneself than in Pūraka or Kumbhaka. There is another point of difference that deserves attention. In case of an average man of health, Pūraka and Kumbhaka, if developed beyond the right proportion, are likely to damage the lungs more than the heart whereas an unduly deep Recaka is likely to affect the heart more than the lungs.[6]

Recaka should always take a longer time than Pūraka. The orthodox proportion between Pūraka and Recaka is 1:2 An attempt should be made to reach this standard. Here again one has to bear in mind that Recaka should never be so prolonged as to make the following inhalation any way hurried. In fact in fixing up the proportions of the component parts of a Prāṇāyāma, that is, of Pūraka, Kumbhaka and Recaka one has to see that one can perform with comfort, not only one Prāṇāyāma, but all the successive Prāṇāyāma also. If at a sitting one wants to go through, say, fourteen rounds of Ujjāyī, one should never feel the need of snatching a normal finish. No undue sense of suffocation should be experienced at any stage in the practice of Prāṇāyāma, whatever the number of rounds that one wants to have at a time. So necessary care is to be taken not only in fixing up the component parts of a single round, but also in fixing up the total number of rounds one wants to go through at one sitting.

Pūraka - (Inhale both Nostril, Contract the glotties with Sobbing Sound)

6. For exhaustive explanation read Ujjāyī Prāṇāyāma Explained in *Yoga-Mīmāṃsā, Vol. IV.*

Kumbhaka - (Pause with bandhas)

Rechaka - (Exale Left Nostril with double time)

The Total Duration of a Single Round

This will necessarily depend upon the capacity of every man. Without giving our reasons here we may state the following rules :

(i) A spiritual culturist should try to prolong the duration of each round.

(ii) A physical culturist who looks to the oxygen value alone of the performance, should try to shorten the duration of each round.

(iii) A physical culturist who looks to the other values in addition to the oxygen value, should try to have four rounds a minute.

Concentration

A spiritual culturist should concentrate his attention upon that point in the nasal part of his pharynx where the first touch of the inhaled air is felt. This point is situated just behind the anterior openings of the nasal passages, in the dome of the nasal pharynx, directly above the top of the arch formed by the junction of the hard and soft palates. In exhalation the last touch of the exhaled air will be felt at this very point. Concentration on this point is to be maintained throughout Prāṇāyāma whether one is doing Pūraka, Kumbhaka or Recaka.

A physical culturist should concentrate his attention upon the air he breathes. During inhalation and exhalation it should be marked at the glottis as it meets with friction there. During Kumbhaka the concentration should be on the air held in the chest.

In this connection there are many other points of importance both for the physical and spiritual culturists. But the scope of the present handbook precludes the possibility of any reference to them here.

General Hints

As stated in the last chapter a beginner, whether he is physical culturist or spiritual culturist, will practise Ujjāyī without Kumbhaka. For the former, Kumbhaka is not necessary unless he wants to perform such feats of strength as are exhibited by Prof. Rāmāmūrti and his imitators. Even for a spiritual culturist the need of Kumbhaka arises after a good deal of progress. At any rate a novice should avoid Kumbhaka for some day at least and when it is to be taken up, utmost care should be taken against undue strain.

There is another point which we shall recommend to our readers. Even in Ujjāyī. Recaka may be practised with both the nostrils. We know that this change is not in keeping with the orthodox technique, but it will be found very convenient by beginners. Again we do not think that this change will much affect the expected results.

In case this recommendation is taken up and also that of dropping out Kumbhaka, there remains no need of using the right hand for closing the nostrils.

What should be the total number of rounds to be practised daily and how should these rounds be distributed ?

For a spiritual culturist the maximum number of rounds is 320.

This is to be distributed over two to four sittings according to one's convenience. A physical culturist satisfy himself with a total of 240 to be finished in two installments. For him the morning and evening hours are the best.

By both the types of Yogic culturists, a beginning can be made with seven rounds at each instalment, adding three rounds to each instalment per week. For several years we have found this to be a very safe programme, the same having been tried in thousands of cases.

The whole treatment accorded to the subject here, is from the point of view of an average man of health. People not suffering from any serious trouble either of the heart or of the lungs, can also follow these instructions with suitable changes. But any one suffering from a pulmonary or cardiac disorder, is strictly warned against taking to these practices on his own responsibility. He must consult an expert.

CHAPTER V

KAPĀLABHĀTI

The Name

THE word Kapālabhāti is a compound consisting of two members: Kapāla and Bhāti. In Sanskrit Kapāla means the *skull*, and Bhāti is derived from a Sankrit root meaning to *shine*. Hence, Kapālabhāti means an *exercise that makes the skull shining*. Kapālabhāti is one of the six cleansing processes, known in Haṭha Yoga as Shat Kriyās[1] and is intended to clear the nasal passages *contained in the skull*, along with the remaining parts of the respiratory system. As the exercise necessarily cleanses a part[2] of the skull, the name Kapālabhāti is appropriately given to it.

---

1. The following verse enumerates the six cleansing processes :

   धौतिर्वस्तिस्तथा नेतिस्त्राटकं नौलिकं तथा ।

   कपालभातिश्चैतानि षट् कर्माणि प्रचक्षते ।। H.P. II 22

   Out of these six, धौति (Vol, II pp. 170-177) वस्ति (Vol I, 99 101-104) and नौलि (Vol I pp 25-26 and Vol IV pp 320-234) have been treated at some length in the journal, *Yoga-Mīmāṃsā*.

2. We are studying the physiology of Kapālbhāti in our laboratory. The research work is yet far too incomplete to enable us to make a definite statement. But the little work that has already been donc in this connection, has led us to think that the exercise is capable of cleansing not only the respiratory system but also the different parts of the human anatomy connected with the skull. We have also reason to believe that Kapākbhāti is capable of cleansing even the capillaries of the remotest parts of the human body.

In Yoga Śāstra[3] three different varieties of Kapālabhāti have been mentioned. All these varieties are characterized in common by their capacity to cleanse the nasal passages contained in the skull. Here, however, we are going to notice most popular variety of the lot. As will be seen from its technique, this variety is a type of breathing[4] exercise

The Technique[5]

Although Kapālabhāti is not[6] a Prāṇāyāma in the strictly technical sense of the word, it is surely a breathing exercise and as such all that is said about the place, the seat, the time etc., in chapter III of this handbook applies as much to this exercise as to Prāṇāyāma proper. So the student should select his place, arrange

---

3. Vide *Gheraṇḍa Saṃhitā, 1 55.*
4. The other two varieties are performed with the help of water and constitute what we may call the Yogic nasal douches. In this connection it is to be noted that the technique of the variety discussed in the present handbook is different from the technique as it given by the author of *Gheraṇḍa Saṃhitā.* In writing this chapter, we have followed the author of Haṭha Pradīpikā. The technique given in *Gheraṇḍa Saṃhitā is of little practical value. Hence we have left it out of consideration here.*
5. Readers wishing to practise Kapālabhāti according to the technique given here, are earnestly requested to study carefully what we have written on respiration in chapter I. This will enable them not only to grasp intelligently the different points of the present technique, but also will help them to eliminate all possible errors from their practice of exercise.
6. We will discuss this point later on in this very chapter.

his seat and fix his time according to the general instructions given in that chapter. The next question is to be considered is about the posture appropriate to this exercise. A student of physical culture can assume any sitting posture that is convenient to him. We do not think that Kapālabhāti can be advantageously practised in standing posture. As will be seen later on, this breathing exercise requires a very free movement of the abdominal muscles. Now the front abdominal muscles are not fully relaxed while one is standing, and as such cannot be freely manipulated. But while one is sitting these abdominal muscles can undergo complete relaxation and their movement can be thoroughly controlled in this position. Hence even a physical culturist will do well to practise Kapālabahtī in a sitting posture.

The question of a spiritual culturist stands on a different footing. He is very strongly recommended the Lotus Pose (*Vide* p. 30), for the practice of Kapālabhāti. The reason is this : Kapālabhāti to be of any spiritual advantage, has to be practised vigorously and over a good length of time. A vigorous practice of Kapālabhāti, even for a few minutes, makes almost every tissue in the human body vibrate. These vibrations become more and more violent if the exercise is pushed further with the original vigour, till at last it becomes very difficult to control the pose that one may have assumed. Now out of the meditative poses[7] that we have recommended to the students of spiritual culture, Padmāsana is

7. Siddha, Svastika and Sama are the other meditative poses recommended to a student of spiritual culture. For the physiology of these meditative poses read our article on the subject in *Yoga-Mīṃāṃsā, Vol. III*

the only sitting pose that can keep the limbs of the student in their proper place under such circumstances. The principal question is of the lower extremities. The foot-lock which forms part of the Padmāsana technique is so arranged that no amount of violence done to the legs can unlock it. In other meditative poses, the legs are loose, and the violent jerks which the body begins to receive through vigorous Kapālabhāti, soon throw them out of order. As it is essential that the pose once assumed is maintained intact throughout the exercise, Padmāsana is the only meditative pose available for the practice Kapālabhāti.

This traditional and rational teaching of Kapābhāti being practised in Padmāsana only, is supported by the author of Haṭha Pradīpikā. We must admit that Svātmārāma Sūri does not say in so many words that Padmāsana is obligatory, for the practice of Kapābhāti but we can know what he means from what the says in connection with Bhastrikā. Whereas in the case of other Kumbhakas, Svātmārāma does not mention any particular pose, in his description of the technique of the Bhastrikā Kumbhaka he makes a special mention of Padmāsana.[8] This means that according to him the Bhastrikā Kumbhaka must be practised in the Lotus

---

8. His description of the technique of Bhastrikā opens as follows : -
सम्यक् पद्मासनं बद्धा .. .. । H.P.II 59
(Having satisfactorily taken the Lotus pose...)

Pose.[9] Now the exercise of Kapālabhāti is so akin to Bhastrikā, that we can safely say that Bhastrikā[10] is equal to Kapālabhāti plus a Kumbhaka of the Ujjāyī type. That being the case we can logically conclude that Āsana which is obligatory for Bhastrikā is also obligatory for Kapālabhāti.[11]

---

9. This very conclusion has been drawn by Svātmārāma's commentator Brahmānanda. The latter says : - भस्त्राकुंभकस्य पद्मासनपूर्वकमेवानुष्ठानात्तदादौ पद्मासनमाह । (The author describes the Lotus Pose before giving the technique of the Bhastrā (the same as Bhastrikā) Kumbhaka, because that pose is obligatory for that type of Kumbhaka.)

10. Our readers will better understand this statement when they will have read the next chapter which discusses the technique of Bhastrikā.

11. For the guidance of the practical students of Yoga we may mention here that even for spiritual purposes Kapālabhāti may be practised in some other meditative pose, provided it is not done so vigorously not for so long a time as to induce violent jerks. There are many people who find it very difficult, if not altogether impossible, to have the foot-lock formed. These need not forego the practice of Kapālabhāti simply because they cannot carry out this part of its technique. They may assume any comfortable sitting posture for this exercise.

It is to be remembered in this connection that the Lotus Pose to be assumed for Kapālabhāti mainly consists of the foot-lock.[12] The position of the hands may, as usual, be either on the knees forming Jñāna-Mudrā, or they may be arranged in front of the abdomen as required in Padmāsana. Regarding the two Bandhas, namely, Jālandhara and Mūla, which ordinarily form part of Padmāsana, the following instructions may be attended to.

In breathing exercises Jālandhara-Bandha has to be practised only during the period of Kumbhaka.[13] Kapābhāti is indeed a breathing exercise but consisting as it does of incessant respiration exclusively, it does not include Kumbhaka. Hence the practice of Jālandhara is not needed in the Lotus Pose when it is taken for Kapālabhāti.

---

12. What we say will be clear when we read Svātmārāma's description of Padmāsana when it is taken for Bhastrikā. He talks there of the foot-lock and nothing else.

    ऊर्वोरुपरि संस्थाप्य शुभे पादतले उभे ।

    पद्मासन भवेदेतत् ... ... ।। H.P.II 58.

    (The lotus Pose is secured when the feet with their clean soles upturned are arranged on the thighs....)

13. There is only one exception to this general rule. That exception is to be found in the technique of the Mūrccha Kumbhaka (Kumbhaka for rendering the mind passive). This Kumbhikā (feminine of Kumbhaka) require the expulsion of breath to be done with a Chin-Lock.

The other, namely, Mūla-Bandha is to be treated in a different way. Students of Yoga peculiarly susceptible to the vibrations set up by Kapālabhāti, *involuntarily* form this Bandha, as the vibrations become more and more violent. The whole pelvic region is *automatically* contracted resulting in the vigorous contraction of the anal sphincters. Hence it is desirable that in the initial stage of the practice, the intentional formation of Mūla- Bandha is avoided. If it is found that the Kapābhāti vibrations do not automatically secure this Bandha, even when a Yogic student is well established in this exercise, Mūla-Bandha may be voluntarily introduced in the technique of this Kriyā.

What has been said about the erect spine in the case of Ujjāyī equally applies to Kapālabhāti.

Having dealt with the Āsana necessary for Kapālabhāti, we now proceed to discuss the technique of the exercise proper.

Broadly speaking Kapālabhāti is a breathing exercise of the abdominal or diaphragmatic[13*] type in which sudden expulsions of breath follow one another in quick succession and which is characterized by the absence of any pause in the movement of breath so long as the exercise continues. So this exercise consists of Recaka and Pūraka only, Kumbhaka being done away with

---

CF. पूरकान्ते गाढतरं बद्ध्वा जालंधरं शनैः ।
रेचयेन्मुर्च्छनाख्येयं ... ... ।। H.P. II 68.

(In the Kumbhikā called Mūrcchanā (the same as Mūrcchā), one should expire slowly while the Chin-Lock is very firmly secured after the completion of inspiration....)

13*. For information on this point read chapter I.

entirely. Again between Recaka and Pūraka, Recaka is the principal part of the practice, Pūraka, being only supplementary. In the case of Kapābhāti there is one more feature which deserves to be borne in mind. In other breathing exercises in *Yoga,* one Pūraka, one Kumbhaka and one Recaka complete one round. But in Kapālabhāti one round consists of as many expulsions of breath as one likes or is capable of performing. Thus one may have several hundred expulsions in a single round of Kapābhāti.

Let us now come to details and let us start with Recaka which constitutes the main feature of the exercise.

Recaka

As in Ujjāyī so in any other breathing exercise, whether Eastern or Western, Recaka and Pūraka are invariably advised to be very deep. In fact Recaka is expected to be so complete that no additional quantity of air could be further extracted from the lungs. So also Pūraka is expected to be so complete that no additional quantity of air could be further introduced into the lungs. Kapālabhāti, however, stands on a different level. It is the only[14] exercise which does not require very deep expiration or very deep inspiration. Then what is the volume of air that is to be expelled from the lungs in an expiratory attempt in Kapālabhāti ? In every Recaka in Kapālabhāti only as much air is to be exhaled as can be driven out of lungs by a sudden and vigorous inward stroke of the front abdominal muscles. Naturally this amount of air will be different

14. Also that part of Bhastrikā which corresponds to Kapālabhāti. It is to be noted, however, that Bhastrikā as a Kumbhaka does require deepest possible Pūraka and Recaka to precede and follow it.

for different individuals. We have conducted experiments in our laboratory to measure these amounts for different subjects and also to compare these with the respective amounts of their normally exhaled air. On the strength of this evidence we can say that in Kapālabhāti the exhalation should be a little deeper than in ordinary breathing. (For example, if the volume of the normally expired air in the case of an individual, is 360 ml., he is expected to exhale about 450 ml. in an expulsion in Kapālabhāti). In everyday practice the following rule of thumb will be sufficient. Let the abdominal stroke be complete and let the breath flow out easily. When this is done the volume of the expired air will take care of itself.

The essence of Recaka, however, does not lie in regulating the volume of the expired air, but it lies in a definite arrangement of the different anatomical parts especially those that are directly involved in breathing. It has already been stated above that Kapālabhāti is an exercise in abdominal breathing. Hence in this exercise exhalation is effected more by the movements of the front abdominal muscles and the diaphragm than by the movements of muscles acting on and between the ribs. In fact the muscles that act on and between the ribs are kept contracted as long as a particular round of Kapālabhāti lasts, whatever the number of expulsions that go to form that round. In other types of breathing exercises in Yoga, these muscles remain contracted only in Pūraka and Kumbhaka. As soon as Recaka begins they are relaxed, the relaxation being complete when Recaka is the deepest. But in Kapālabhāti, owing to its peculiar character, the muscles acting on and between the ribs, once contracted, remain in the same condition, keeping the ribs raised even during expulsions of breath.

The only muscles that freely move throughout the exercise, undergoing alternate contraction and relaxation, are the diaphragm and the front abdominal muscles. This should not be interpreted to mean, that the ribs do not *sink at all* during exhalation in Kapālabhāti. As a matter of fact it is impossible to exhale without a little lowering of the ribs. But the falling of the ribs is so little in a well conducted exercise of Kapālabhāti that it is almost negligible. This can be verified by the external appearance of the thorax. It neither rises nor falls appreciably throughout a round of Kapālabhāti. (For the position of the thorax and the abdomen compare Figs. 40 and 41).

The exercise of Kapālabhāti, as stated above, is a play of the abdominal muscles and the diaphragm. These must be thoroughly supple and capable of undergoing sudden and vigorous contractions. In the Recaka of Kapālabhāti, the front abdominal muscles are suddenly and vigorously contracted giving an inward

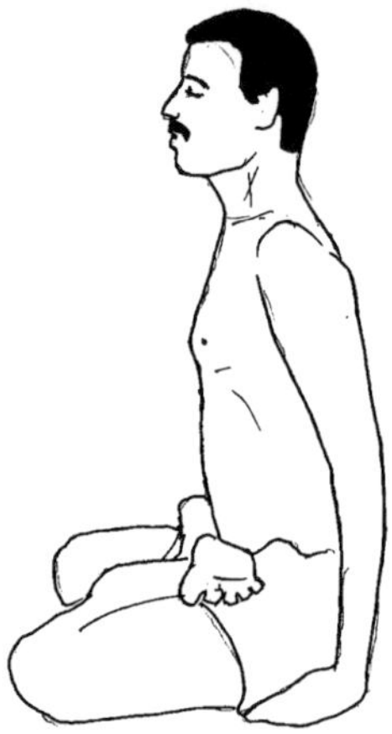

FIG. 40. Abdomen and Thorax at the end of Pūraka in Kapālabhāti

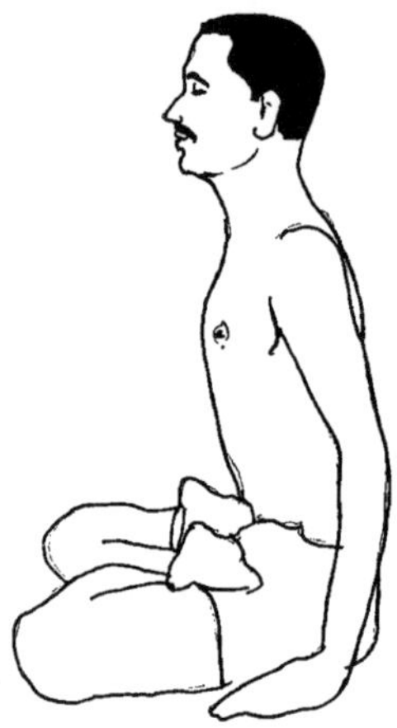

FIG. 41. Abdomen and Thorax at the end of Recaka in Kapālabhāti.

push to the abdominal viscera which in their turn move upward pushing up the relaxing diaphragm that recedes into the thorax expelling a volume of air from the lungs. As the retracting lungs are not allowed to contract the thorax, expiration in Kapālabhāti is not as deep as in Ujjāyī. The speed with which the diaphragm and the abdominal muscles can be manipulated will depend upon one's practice. It is not desirable, however, to develop speed at the cost of thoroughness.

Upto now we have discussed the work to be done with the abdomen and the thorax in Kapābhāti. We now proceed to see how the respiratory passage outside the thorax is to be worked.

In Ujjāyī we are required to close the glottis partially. In the present exercise this is to be avoided. The reason is clear. The volume of air exhaled in a single Recaka of Kapālabhāti is so suddenly expelled, that a partially closed glottis would afford serious obstruction to the passage of the air and would render the expiration incomplete. There is one tradition,[15] however, which would wish very slight narrowing of the glottis even in Kapālabhāti. But the extent to which this is to be done is so small that the expelled air is not likely to be held back to any appreciable extent.

When the expelled air is allowed to escape freely through the glottis, it has a smooth though rapid passage to the end of the nostrils. If permitted to do their work automatically, the nostrils will open out voluntarily to facilitate the flow of the expired air. So the student of Yoga should not try to manage either his nostrils

---

15. This is the tradition followed by the author of Haṭha Pradīpikā

or his facial muscles at this stage. Very often people are in the habit of having all sorts of ugly contortions of their face when they are practising Kapālabhāti. This is far from being desirable. The air should be permitted to have a very smooth escape which it would surely have if allowed to go its own way.

It is to be remembered however, that the rapid expulsion of a volume of air will surely cause some friction at the lower end of the nostrils. But this does not matter. As our readers know, this part of the internal nose is covered with thick skin and any friction there is not likely to lead to any untoward results. What is to be cautiously avoided is the friction of the air with any of the delicate parts of the mucous membrane that lines the interior of the nasal passage.

Pūraka

In order to get a clear grasp of the process of Pūraka in Kapālabhāti, it is desirable for our readers to refresh their memory regarding a few facts about normal respiration. Normally the process of inhalation is active whereas the process of exhalation is passive. In normal inspiration the thorax is to be opened out for increasing its internal capacity, so that its lowered internal pressure might draw in air from outside. Thus the muscles that act on and between the ribs, so also the diaphragm, are put into action and contracted, raising the former and lowering the latter. But normal expiration is only a passive process. The muscles referred to just now are relaxed. Consequently the ribs sink down of themselves and the diaphragm is drawn up by the retracting lungs that voluntarily shrink owing to their elastic recoil. It is only on the side of anterior abdominal muscles that things are a little different. These muscles are active in normal expiration and passive in normal inspiration, because during expiration they contract and during inspiration they stand relaxed. Thus their role in inspiration is just the opposite of the one played by the thoracic muscles.

Now let us return to the process of Pūraka in Kapālabhāti.

As noted above the exercise of Kapālabhāti is a play of the abdominal muscles. The muscles of the thorax are kept contracted throughout the exercise whether it is inhalation that is being practised or exhalation. The thoracic muscles are relaxed only when the exercise is over. It is only the front abdominal muscles that keep on moving to and fro, according as they are contracted for exhalation or relaxed for inhalation. We shall presently consider the case of the diaphragm.

Thus Kapālabhāti being markedly an exercise in abdominal breathing one has to pay attention only to his abdominal muscles. At the end of Recaka these muscles stand contracted. So in Pūraka one has simply to withdraw his control of these muscles and they will relax themselves. Relaxation of muscles is a passive act. So when the abdominal muscles are let go at the end of Recaka, they will voluntarily relax.

Upto now we have left out of consideration one important muscle, the diaphragm. Upto a particular extent the manipulation of this musscle is entirely under the control of our will. But this muscle does not require the exercise of our will for its ordinary movements, just as the other respiratory muscles go on doing their ordinary work, without any attention on our part. While we are deeply absorbed in some work, these respiratory muscles are functioning even without entering into our consciousness.

Now, as stated previously, at the end of Recaka the diaphragm stands relaxed, but ready for another contraction. The stimulus from the inspiratory centre brings about this contraction and the descent of the diaphgram is allowed by the relaxing abdominal muscles. The lowering of the diaphragm increases the vertical diameter of the thorax, the internal pulmonary capacity is increased, and the internal pressure being lowered, the external air moves in, till the air expelled in Recaka is replaced, raising the intra-pulmonary pressure to one atmosphere.

Thus it will be clear that in Pūraka no wilful contraction of muscles is necessary. One has simply to relax his abdominal muscles and Pūraka is performed. That is why we have said that Pūraka in Kapālabhāti is a passive act.

Thus it will be seen that there is a sharp contrast between the Recaka process and the Pūraka process in Kapālabhāti. The former is sudden and vigorous, the latter smooth and quit. In fact Pūraka in Kapālabhāti is there only to provide air for the next expulsion which alone forms the real part of the exercise.

The volume of air inhaled in a single Pūraka must be for all practical purposes equal to the volume of air exhaled in the previous expulsion. The student of Kapālabhāti has however, to remember that the time taken for one Pūraka is not the same as the time taken for one Recaka. If we suppose that one Recaka and one Pūraka taken together require half a second, it may be roughly stated that Recaka would occupy only one-fourth of this total time,

Pūraka occupying the remaining three-fourths. In Pūraka the whole respiratory passage is kept fully open, there being no narrowing of it either at the glottis or any other part. Hence, air glides smoothly into the lungs, we might say almost[16] as smoothly as in normal inspiration.

Recaka and Pūraka are performed in a quick succession, no time being allowed to go by in between any two acts till a round is completed. Pūraka follows Recaka and Recaka follows Pūraka without a break. All the while the noisy and sudden Recaka is so much in evidence that the smooth and quiet Pūraka sinks into nothingness. So in practice, Kapālahāti appears to be an exercise of successive and sudden expulsions only. Each expulsion is preceded by a relaxation of the abdomen and is accompanied by a sudden and vigorous inward stroke of it. The incessant blowing at the nose accompanied by the alternate rise and fall of the abdomen, give the exercise an appearance of the bellows of a village smith.

---

16. The minimum time taken up by an ordinary inspiration is nearly a *second and a half*, whereas inspiration in Kapālabhāti, at an average speed of 120 expulsions per minute, requires only *three-tenths* of a second. Again the volume of air inhaled in Kapālabhāti is slightly larger than that inhaled in ordinary inspiration. Hence we find that the volume of air passing through the respiratory passage *during a particular unit of time* is far larger in Kapālabhati than in ordinary inspiration. Hence inhalation in Kapālabhāti cannot be as smooth as normal inhalation. Still experience will show that Pūraka in Kapālabhāti is smooth enough, and there is no roughness about it, corresponding to one evidenced in Recaka.

In fact that is the simile given by the author of Hatha-Pradipika to illustrate the action of Kapālabhāti.[17]

Rechaka - (Active Exhale with both Nostril)

Pūraka - (Passive Inhale with both Nostril)

A Single Round in Kapālabhāti

Upto this time we have considered the technique of an individual exhalation and an individual inhalation in Kapālabhāti. Now we wish to discuss the measure of single round of Kapālabhāti and also to see how that round should begin and end.

In determining the measure of round, we have to determine the number of expulsions that go to form one round and the speed with which these expulsions are performed. The question of speed we shall take up later on. First we shall say something about the number of expulsions. In this connection we can follow the golden rule laid down by an old Sanskrit proverb[18] according to which a humble beginning is always free from danger. The number of

---

17. Svatmarama Suri say s:-

 भस्त्रावल्लोहकारस्य रेचपूरौ ससंभ्रमौ ।

 कपालभातिविंख्याता ... ... ।। H.P.II 35

 (Hurried exhalations and inhalations after the fashion of an iron-smith's bellows, constitute the famous exercise of Kapālabhāti...) It is interesting to note here that Kapālabhāti play such a prominent part in the Bhastrā or Bhastrikā Kumbhaka, that Kumbhaka gets the very name of bellows. Bhastrā or Bhastrikā means bellows in Sanskrit.

18. अल्पारम्भः क्षेमकरः ।

expulsions in each round which we prescribe to our patients[19] and even to students of physical or spiritual[20] culture is eleven to begin with. Generally three rounds are given at each sitting, two settings being advised per day, one in the morning and the other in the evening. In normal cases eleven expulsions are added to each round every week, till at last round consists of one hundred and twenty-one expulsions.

Every round should begin with an exhalation and should end with an inhalation. In between any two successive rounds normal respiration should be allowed to intervene. It will be found that this intervening respiration is unusually slow and smooth.[21] This period affords the rest necessary for the respiratory system in general and the abdominal muscles in particular. The length of this period should be settled according to one's own convenience. Generally speaking half a minute to one minute should be sufficient for preparing one for the next round. The dose of Kapālabhāti prescribed in the last two paragraphs is perfectly general. It is intended for an average man of health and is sufficiently strong for bringing about the *physiological* results expected of this

---

19. Whether Kapālabhāti can be prescribed to a particular patient and whether a change in this measure is indicated by the condition of his health are questions which cannot be detailed here. The discussion offered in these pages is from the point of view of an average man of health.
20. Although Kapālabhāti is not a pranayamic exercise, it is of considerable spiritual value.
21. A general explanation of this phenomenon will be found in this chapter under *General Hints*.

exercise. Those who feel themselves above the average, may have a larger measure of Kapālabhāti in their daily practice. For the purposes of physical culture, we might recommend double the average dose as the maximum. This doubling may be secured either by doubling the expulsions in each round, keeping the number of rounds constant or by doubling the number of rounds, keeping the number of expulsions in each round constant. Needless to say that the latter course will put less strain on the system than the former. The need of a spiritual culturist is greater. He may have, for his maximum dose, three rounds of three minutes each, at a sitting. It is absolutely *necessary, however,* that in reaching *this maximum no undue strain is put upon the system*. To be spiritually useful, the practice should set up the vibrations to which we have made reference in discussing the propriety of the Lotus Pose in this exercise.[22] These vibrations are set up only after *prolonged rounds*. Hence a spiritual culturist should distribute his total measure of the Kapālabhāti exercise in as small a number of rounds as possible. Even in doing this the question of undue strain should never be lost sight of.

Concentration

The question of concentration is of supreme importance to a student of spiritual culture in his practice of Kapālabhāti. With every expulsion of breath, he is delivering inward strokes upon the abdominal viscera. He is to think that these strokes are being delivered

---

22. Vide pp. 63-34.

against a centre in the lower abdomen in which spiritual energy[23] is stored up. This concentration, if maintained throughout the exercise, will enable a student[24] to make some centre of his nervous system spiritually active.[25] Even during the period of rest that is taken in between two successive rounds, the spiritual culturist should entertain no other thought except the working up of the desired centre.[26]

---

23. According to Yogic teachings, as stated in chapter II, Kuṇḍalinī which represents spirityal energy is coiled up in the lower abdomen. The concentration being prescribed is calculated to wake up this Kuṇḍalinī. We have purposely avoided any modern anatomical terms here, simply because we cannot venture any speculative theory in connection with Kuṇḍalinī.

24. We do not wish to raise false hopes. So we request every student of spiritual culture to remember constantly the following fact. The ability to awaken nerve-centres of spiritual value, varies very widely with different individuals. One person may get a response from one of these centres with less than month's active work whereas another person may fail to get it even after six years' labour. So when one wants to embark on a voyage that leads to the land that is beyond all darkness, one should consider himself to be the least qualified of the spiritual aspirants and be prepared for the arduous task before him. This will avoid frequent disappointments and early clamouring for results, provided always that the aspirant has undying faith in the immortal teaching of Bhagavān Śrikṛṣṇa that no spiritual aspirant ever comes to grief.

25. This activity is experienced first in the form of *throbbing* and then in the form of *serene light* glowing at the particular centre.

26. The concentration described in this paragraph is only one of the different concentrations available for Kapālabhāti in spiritual culture. We cannot notice the other concentrations in this handbook for want of space.

The question of a physical culturist is comparatively simple. He should concentrate upon the expulsion, all the while realizing that he is eliminating very large quantities of carbon dioxide and absorbing into his system similarly[27] large quantities of oxygen. This is rendering his blood richer in quality and consequently he is rebuilding the tissues all over his body. These thoughts should accompany not only his expulsions but also his period of rest.

General Hints

As an exercise of very great oxygen value, Kapālabhāti has no parallel. Its nerve culture value is also very great. Its effects upon the circulatory and digestive systems are of considerable physiological importance. The massage of the abdominal viscera which the exercise effects is obvious. The massage of the other anatomical parts though not so clear to an untrained eye, is not of lesser consequence. Even this bare statement of the physiological importance of this exercise should be sufficient to prove that the exercise deserves a definite place in the daily physical culture programme of every man that cares for his health.

All the physiological advantages enumerated in the last paragraph accrue also to a student of spiritual culture. But he practises Kapalabhati for these advantages only up to a particular

27. Generally slightly larger than those of carbon dioxide eliminated.

stage[28] of development. Afterwards Kapalabhati is practised by him for nerve culture and especially for wakening particular nerve-centres of spiritual significance.

There is, however, another way in which a spiritual culturist takes advantages Kapālabhāti of for his higher development. He uses Kapālbhāti for enabling him to practise his Prāṇāyāma more efficiently. We shall now state briefly how this is done. The exercise of Kapālabhāti leads to the elimination of carbon dioxide from the system on very large scale. The absorption of oxygen into the system is also abnormally large. This extraordinarily heavy exchange of gases in the lungs brought about by Kapālabhāti, together with the influence this practice exerts on particular nerves, soon establishes such metabolic conditions in the body as lead to slow down respiration and thus enable a yogic student to have a greater control over his lungs.[29]

It is a common experience of the students of Prāṇāyāma, that their attempts to control the lungs are seriously interfered with by the respiratory centre. A strong stimulus coming from this centre, makes hasty inspiration or expiration obligatory. If, however, the respiratory centre could be so quietened as to send out feeble

---

28. As stated in the beginning of this chapter Kapālabhāti is one of the six cleansing process advised in Yoga for securing what is technically called Nāḍīśuddhi that is, the physiological balance necessary for spiritual development. Nāḍiśuddhi literally means the purification of nerves. This attainment of Nāḍīśuddhi indicates the stage where Kapālabhāti ceases to be practised for physiological advantage by a spiritual culturist.
29. For information on this point read chapter I.

impulses, if at all, the interference of this centre with our Prāṇāyāmic exercises would be the least, and we could manage the measure of our Pūraka, Kumbhaka and Recaka as we pleased. This quieting of the respiratory centre is brought about by Kapālabhāti in the manner explained in the last paragraph. That is why students of Prāṇāyāma are able to perform their pranayamic exercises more efficiently, if they are prefixed by a few rounds of Kapālabhāti. That is why Yogic tradition requires a student of Yoga to practise Kapālabhāti before starting with Prāṇāyāma proper,[30] in his daily course of exercises.

We cannot close this chapter without discussing the question of speed with which the exercise is to be gone through.

As a cautious measure one can start at the rate of one expulsion per second. This may be developed into two expulsions per second in due course of time. One hundred and twenty expulsions per minute should be considered to be a fairly good speed for an average man of health. Those that feel themselves to be above the average may develop two hundred expulsions per minute. To exceed this limit would be physically impossible because then the expirations begin to be so slow that the exercise would lose all its efficacy. A tolerable good speed is essential for Kapālabhāti to be spiritually useful.

---

30. It is to be remembered that students of spiritual culture practise Prāṇāyāma for the culture of their nerves. This is done by the manipulation of particular muscles, especially the diaphragm. Therefore, these students want to be free to manage their diaphragm as they please. This they are able to do when interference from the respiratory centre is largely eliminated.

The vigour of expulsions is a thing to be constantly attended to. Any attempt to develop speed at the cost of vigour is in the wrong direction.

The degree of vigour and speed, the measure of single round, the number of rounds to be done at one sitting and the total amount of exercise to be done in a day, are things which should be cautiously and judicially determined. Kapālabhāti is a vigorous exercise and therefore less innocent than Ujjāyī. Hence, the necessity of being very careful in getting the right sort of dose. We shall close this chapter by repeating here what we have said at the end of the preceding chapter.

The whole treatment accorded to the subject here, is from the point of view of an average man of health. People not suffering from any serious trouble either of the heart or of the lungs, can also follow these instructions with suitable changes. But any one suffering from pulmonary or cardiac disorder, is strictly warned against taking to these practices on his own responsibility. He must consult an expert.

CHAPTER VI

BHASTRIKĀ

The Name

By this time our readers have become familiar with the meaning of the word Prāṇāyāma.[1] They have also seen that Svāmārāma Sūri, the reputed author of *Haṭha Pradīpikā,* recognizes eight[2] varieties of Prāṇāyāma of which Bhastrikā is one. A reference has already been made to the meaning[3] of the word Bhastrikā and also to the technique[4] of it. In this chapter we shall study this Prāṇāyāma at some length.

In Sanskrit, Bhastrikā means bellows. This Prāṇāyāma is called Bhastrikā because it is characterized by incessant and quick expulsions of breath in all its varieties,[5] imitating the actively hissing bellows of a village smith. Whether in these expulsions both the nostrils are used as in the last two vaieties, the first two varieties, or only one nostril is used as in the last two varieties, is all immaterial, quick succession of forceful expiration is the most

---

1. *Vide* pp. 35-37
2. *Vide* p. 38
3. *Vide* foot-note 17, p. 69.
4. *Vide* pp. 63-64
5. There are as may as four varieties of this Prāṇāyāma. We are going to notice all of them in this chapter.

prominent feature of every type of Bhastrikā. Hence,[6] the name.

The Technique

Those of our readers that may have made themselves thoroughly familiar with the technique of Ujjāyī and Kapālabhāti, will find almost nothing new to learn in the technique of Bhastrikā, at least so far as the first two varieties are concerned. We shall presently see why this is so.

First Variety[7] : The first part of this variety is completely identical with the exercise of Kapālabhāti as it is described in the last chapter. The breathing is entirely abdominal, the ribs being raised and kept up in that condition by the continued slight contraction of the intercostals. Both the nostrils are used for forceful and quick expulsions of breath that follow one another in rapid succession. Inhalations are passive being brought about by the realization of the abdominal muscles. In fact this part of Bhastrikā is nothing more than the practice of Kapālabhāti.

---

6. Svātmārāma Sūri says : - -

   पुनर्विरेचयेत्तद्वत्पूरयेच्च पुनः पुनः ।
   यथैव लोहकारेण भस्त्रा वेगेन चाल्यते ।।
   तथैव स्वशरीरस्थं चालयेत्पवनं धिया । ... ... ।। H.P. II. 61.

   (One should exhale again, so also inhale again, doing the same repeatedly. Just as a blacksmith works his bellows actively, so should one move his physical breath with speed and attention.)

7. This is the type of Bhastrikā traditionally handed down to the Director of the *Kaivalyadhāma* and daily practised by the Sādhakas of the Āśrama. The author of *Gheraṇḍa-Saṃhitā* recommends this variety to the students of Yoga, Vide Lesson, V, pp. 75-77

After a number of exhalation, this number[8] being determined by the strength of the individual practising Prāṇāyāma, deepest possible Pūraka is made as in the case of Ujjāyī. Air is inhaled through both the nostrils and the abdominal muscles are kept controlled. Only the partial closure of the glottis and the consequent frictional sound produced in inspiration are to be avoided. The glottis is to be kept fully open. The air is to be drawn in by *slowly* expanding the chest. The passage of the inspired air through the nose and throat is to be so gentle, that no friction is caused in any part of the respiratory tract. It is desirable that the process of Pūraka should cover at least eight seconds.

Pūraka is followed by Kumbhaka. The inspired air is retained by completely closing the glottis and by securing Jālandhara Bandha. The closing of the nostrils with the fingers as in Ujjāyī is necessary. In fact Kumbhaka in Bhastrikā is to be practised exactly as Kumbhaka in Ujjāyī, the two Kumbhakas being thoroughly identical in every detail, including the control of the abdominal muscles.

Recaka follows Kumbhaka. Except for the partial opening of the glottis and the resulting soft sound of a low pitch, Recaka in Bhastrikā is quite similar to Recaka in Ujjāyī. As in Pūraka so in Recaka, Bhastrikā requires the glottis to be thoroughly open, so that the returning air from the lungs may smoothly glide by. We

---

8. In *Gheraṇḍa-Saṃhitā only twenty expulsions of breath have been advised. In the cultural and curative work done in the Āśrama, we have found that the measures of Kapālabhāti and Bhastrikā agree with each other with wonderful accuracy. Also read the* General *Hints* given at the end of this chapter.

have already studied the technique of Recaka in Ujjāyī. In Bhastrikā the same steps are taken to start and to complete Recaka. First the hold on the nostrils is removed,[9] then Jālandhara-Bandha is unlocked, afterwards the glottis is thrown open, and lastly by simultaneous contraction of the chest and abdomen the air is slowly sent out of the recoiling lungs.

The Pūraka and Recaka that respectively and immediately precede and follow Kumbhaka in Bhastrikā Prāṇāyāma, differ from those Pūraka and Recaka which succeed each other without the interruption of Kumbhaka and which form the first part of this exercise corresponding to the practice of Kapālabhāti. Inhalations and exhalations that successively follow each other are shallow, but the inhalation and exhalation that immediately precede and follow Kumbhaka are made the deepest possible of their type.

We shall now sum up this description of a single round of Bhastrikā which consists of two parts, the first being exactly similar to Kapālabhāti and the second roughly similar to Ujjāyī. The student begins with quick expulsions of breath following one another in rapid succession. When the necessary number of expulsions is done, the last expulsion is followed by deepest possible inhalation. After retaining his breath till he could do it comfortably, he exhales as deeply as possible. The end of this deep Recaka completes one round of Bhastrikā.

A few normal breaths for rest and the student is again ready for another round of this Prāṇāyāma.

---

9. As will be stated later on the right hand removed from the nose is again to be placed on the right knee.

Regarding the relative measures of Pūraka, Kumbhaka and Recaka forming the second part of Bhastrikā Prāṇāyāma, and the absolute measure of Kumbhaka therein, what we have said in the chapter on Ujjāyī also holds good here.

The author of *Gheraṇḍa-Saṃhitā* recommends three rounds of Bhastrikā for a man to keep himself fit. In our Āśram we follow this very recommendation and find that an average man of health can keep up his health by practising three rounds of Bhastrikā daily.[10]

Kapalbhati with both Nostril +

1) **Pūraka** - (Inhale both Nostril)
2) **Kumbhaka** - (Pause with bandhas)
3) **Rechaka** - (Exhale Left Nostril)

In short - 20 stroks Kapalbhati + 1 Round Ujjayi type breething = 1 Round Bhastrika

Second Variety[11] : We shall consider this variety in its two parts separately. Starting with the first part which corresponds to Kapālabhāti, we notice that there is a difference in the arrangement

---

10. This is not to be interpreted to mean that an average man of health can always find himself fit simply for practising three rounds of Bhastrikā every day. What our statement means is this. In a well-balanced scheme of Yogic exercises, three rounds of Bhastrikā form a suitable item. Such a scheme was published in *Yoga-Mīṃāṃsā* a few years ago and is to be found in one of the appendices in his handbook. The scheme is being practised all over India by several Yogic culturists on the recommendation of The Āśrama.
11. This variety is recommended by the author of *Haṭha Pradīpikā.*

of the glottis during respiration. The glottis is to be slightly contracted so that a frictional sound is produced while breath is expelled or taken in, but no substantial obstruction, is offered to the passage of the air.[12] This slight contraction of the glottis once secured is to be maintained throughout this part of the exercise. Except for this difference, the first part of this type of Bhastrikā is completely identical with Kapālabhāti.[13]

12. Read foot-note on p. 68 and the paragraph to which it is appended.
13. In making this statement, we have followed the text of *Haṭha Pradīpikā* and not its commentary by Brahmānanda. The commentator is of the opinion that even in the first part of this exercise only one nostril is to be used as will be described in the third and fourth varieties, and not both. We positively know that there are traditions in Southern India which conform to the descriptions of the third and fourth varieties of Bhastrikā as noticed there and as recommended by Brahmānanda in his commentary. But this does not mean that his interpretation of the original text is correct. We shall give our reasons in brief for our difference of opinion.

    The original text relating to inhalation and exhalation in the first part of Bhastrikā runs as follows :-

    मुखं संयम्य यत्नेन प्राणं घ्राणेन रेचयेत् ।। H.P. II 59

    वेगेन पूरयेच्चापि ... ... ।। H.P. II 60

    (Shut up your mouth. Make a forced expiration through the nose and then quickly inhale).

    Here the singular number of the word घ्राणेन has given an opportunity to the commentator to get support from the original text for his varieties of Bhastrikā-the third and the fourth--which alone he recognizes. He explains घ्राणेन as घ्राणस्यैकतरेण रन्ध्रेण (Through one hole in the nose) Now Svāmārāma Sūri whenever he has to make a reference to one nostril or to both the nostrils either to be used alternately, invariably gives specific instructions to that effect. Since no such instructions are given here, we have to take घ्राणेन to

The measure[14] of expirations in the first part of this variety agrees in toto with the measure of expirations in the corresponding part of the preceding variety. With the last expulsion of breath the second part begins.

The second part of this variety is similar to the second part of the first variety except one detail. Here the deep inhalation and exhalation which respectively precedes and follows Kumbhaka are done through one nostril only instead of through both the nostrils as in the previous case. The nostril to be used for inhalation is always the right, whereas that to be used for exhalation is invariably the opposite one. Thus after the last expulsion of breath completing the first part of the exercise, deepest possible inspiration is made through the right nostril. Breath is retained

---

mean *through the nose, that is, through both the nostrils.* The singular number of घ्राणेन need not present any difficulty, as Brahmānanda himself has explained that word elsewhere as *through both the nostrils.* In commenting upon घ्राणेन occurring in Lesson II 53, he writes as follows: घ्राणनैव नासिकयैवेत्यनेनोभाभ्यां नासापुटाभ्यां रेचकः कार्य इत्युक्तम् । So we find that the original text describes the second variety of Bhastrikā, but the commentator tries to find in that text descriptions of the third and the fourth varieties, simply because he advocates the latter two and does not favour the former.

There are additional arguments in support of the view we have taken. But we abstain from quoting them here.

14. Svātmārāma Sūri does not define this measure by putting a numerical restriction upon it. He is of opinion that the bodily strength of an individual should determine his or her measure in every case. He says :- यदा श्रमो भवेद्देहे ... ... ।। H.P. II 62 (When the physical frame is fatigued (the second part should start)).

according to the technique given in the first variety and then it is driven out, the expiration again being as thorough as possible. Needless to say that in this part of the practice the right hand[15] will all along be on the nose to regulate the passage of air. With deepest exhalation after Kumbhaka one round is finished. In order to be ready for the next round, the right hand is returned to its original position on the knee and a few normal breaths are taken.

Under the second variety, we have described only those features which distinguish it from the first. As all other features are entirely identical, for understanding them we refer our readers to what has been said about them under the first variety.

Kapalbhati with both Nostril +
(Contraction of the glottis)

1) **Pūraka** - (Inhale Right Nostril)
2) **Kumbhaka** - (Pause with bandhas)
3) **Rechaka** - (Exhale Left Nostril)

In short - 20 stroks Kapalbhati + 1 Round Suryabhedan = 1 Round Bhastrika

Third Variety : Here again it is desirable to consider the variety in two parts, the first part corresponding to Kapālabhāti and the second corresponding to Ujjāyī. The only difference in Kapālabhāti and the first part of the third variety is that in Kapālabhāti both the nostrils are used for the expulsion of breath, but in this variety of Bhastrika only one nostril is used. Naturally the other nostril is to be kept closed, this closing being effected by the fingers arranged as in the case of Ujjāyī. According to

15. For the exact position of the hand and use of finger read the general instructions given in chapter IV; pp. 53-54.

Brahmānanda for every odd round of Bhastrikā the right nostril is to be used and for every even round the other. Thus breath will be expelled and taken after the fashion of Kapālabhāti through the right nostril in the first, third, fifth and every succeeding odd round of this Prāṇāyāma whereas the expirations and inspiration will be done through the left nostril in the second, fourth, sixth and every even round that follows.

The second part of this variety corresponds exactly with the second part of the last variety, with only one exception. In the second variety the deep inspirations and expirations immediately preceding and following Kumbhaka are invariably done through the right and the left nostrils respectively. But in the third variety, the deep inhalation is to be done through the right nostril in every odd round and through the left nostril in every even round, the deep exhalation being effected invariably through the opposite nostril. Thus in the first, third, fifth and every succeeding odd round, the right nostril will be used for deep inhalation and the left for the deep exhalations, of course after the intermediate Kumbhaka. But in the second, fourth, sixth, and every even round that follow, the left nostril will be used for deep inspiration and the opposite one for deep expiration.

In short the technique of the third variety can be described as follows. Incessant respirations are started through the right nostril, keeping closed the left. When the necessary[16] number of respirations is gone through, deep inspiration is made through the same nostril. After retaining breath according to one's measure, it is fully expelled through the left nostril. This completes the first

16. What number is necessary will be presently stated.

round. The second round commences with forceful expirations as in Kapālabhāti, using for this work the same nostril that was used for the last deep expiration, namely, the left. After due respirations, deep inspiration is made through that very nostril. Breath is retained and let our thoroughly the right nostril. This completes the second round. Thereafter every odd round resembles the first and every even round resembles the second.

As throughout this exercise, in the first as well as in the second part of it, either one or both the nostrils are required to be kept closed, the right hand is always kept on the nose but the left hand is allowed to be on the knee. The fixing up of the chest, the play of the abdominal muscles and the arrangement of the glottis, thoroughly conform to the technique of the first variety.

Regarding the number of expulsions constituting the first part of every round and the total number of rounds that an individual should perform every day, what we have said in this connection in the first variety also applies to this variety.[17]

First Round

(i) Kapalbhati Right Nostril +

1) **Pūraka** - (Inhale with Right Nostril)

2) **Kumbhaka** - (Pause with bandhas)

3) **Rechaka** - (Exhale with Left Nostril)

Second Round

(i) Kapalbhati Left Nostril +

1) **Pūraka** - (Inhale with Left Nostril)

2) **Kumbhaka** - (Pause with bandhas)

3) **Rechaka** - (Exhale with Right Nostril)

---

17. Also read the *General Hints* given at the end of this chapter.

Fourth Variety : In this variety the second part is the same as in the third but the first part differs. Here the first part resembles the second part with two points of difference. In the first part, there is no Kumbhaka and breathing is not deep. Otherwise the two parts are exactly similar. Thus if a particular nostril is used for inspiration, the opposite is used for expiration as is always done in the second part. In simple words the technique may be put down as follows.

Quick inspiration through the right nostril is immediately followed by quick expiration through the left nostril. This chain of incessant inspirations and expirations is prolonged till the individual feels healthy fatigued. That constitutes the first part of the first round. This is followed by the deepest possible inspiration through the right nostril, the necessary retention of breath and the final expiration through the left nostril, which completes the second part of that round and also the round itself. Then the second round commences with quick inspirations through the left[18] nostril, and expirations through the right. In the second part, Pūraka is done through the same nostril as in the first part, that is, through the left, and after due Kumbhaka, Recaka is done through the right nostril.

As in the third variety so in this, the first round is a model for every succeeding odd rounds and the second for every succeeding even rounds.

What we have said about the measures of the first three varieties applies to this type of Bhastrikā also.

---

18. The same through which Recaka of the previous round was done.

Forth Variety

First Round

(i) Kapalbhati with alternate Nostril - Right to Left +

1) **Pūraka** - (Inhale with Right Nostril)

2) **Kumbhaka** - (Pause with bandhas)

3) **Rechaka** - (Exhale with Left Nostril)

Second Round

(ii) Kapalbhati with alternate Nostril - Left to Right +

1) **Pūraka** - (Inhale with Left Nostril)

2) **Kumbhaka** - (Pause with bandhas)

3) **Rechaka** - (Exhale with Right Nostril)

Important Note :

Performing Kumbhaka

follow the sequence

1) Close glottis after Inhale

2) Jalandhar Bandha

3) Close both Nostril

Releasing Kumbhaka

1) Open the appropriate Nostril

2) Release Jalandhar Bandha

3) Open the glottis end exhale

If we examine all the varieties of Bhastrika we find that the first part consists of a quick succession of Recaka and Pūrakas an in Kapālabhāti and the other part consists of deep Pūraka, Kumbhaka and deep Recaka as in Ujjāyī. This is why we have said that Bhastrikā is equal to Kapālabhāti plus Ujjāyī.

Kapālabhāti plays such a prominent part in Bhastrikā that whatever we have said[19] regarding Āsana appropriate to Kapālabhāti applies to this exercise also. Thus a physical culturist should practise Bhastrikā while sitting and a spiritual culturist should always take the Lotus Pose throughout the practice of this Prāṇāyāma. While sitting in Padmāsana whether the hands are arranged as is required by the technique of that posture or whether they are to rest on the knees forming what is called noted, however, that throughout the third and the fourth varieties and during the second part of the first and the second varieties, the right hand has to manage the nostrils and cannot keep company with the left which invariably enjoys the privileged position of resting either on the knee or on the heels arranged in front of the abdomen. The two Bandhas, namely, Mūla and Jālandhara have a place in the technique of this Prāṇāyāma as they form a part of Padmāsana. As regards the former we might at once say that instructions given for its formation etc., in Kapālabhāti apply *in to to* the case of Bhastrikā. We have, however, pointed out that Jālandhara Bandha has no place in Kapālabhāti for obvious reasons. The case of Bhastrikā stands on different footing. Being a Prāṇāyāma, it is to be remembered, however, that Mūla may be maintained throughout the succession of different rounds, but Jālandhara is to be used at the time of Jñāna-Mudrā is left to the choice of the individual. It must be Kumbhaka only, otherwise the neck is to be kept erect.

For knowing the place, seat, time etc., suitable to the practice of Bhastrikā, we refer the readers to chapter III.

---

19. See opening paragraphs of the technique of Kapālabhāti in chapter V.

Concentration

Concentration to be practised in Bhastrikā does not differ from the one recommended under Kapālabhāti for both the types of Yogic culture, spiritual as well as physical.

General Hints

Something has already been said under each variety of Bhastrikā regarding its average measure. The following discussion is intended to make this question of measure clearer to the readers and to suggest progressive plans for their choice.

We have laid down the following equation :

Ujjāyī plus Kapālabhāti is equal to Bhastrikā. Does it mean that the exercise of Bhastrikā can singly replace the two exercises of Ujjāyī and Kapālabhāti ? Yes, theoretically it can but in practice it is not desirable to do so. We shall consider the cases of physical and spiritual culturists separately.

In our discussion on Ujjāyī, we have advised a physical culturist to avoid Kumbhaka at least in the beginning. The same advice holds good even in regard to Bhastrikā. So a beginner when he starts with Bhastrikā as a measure of physical culture, starts without Kumbhaka, and will have eleven expulsions of breath followed by one deep inspiration and one deep expiration. Of these he will have three rounds. Thus in all there will be thirty-three expirations of the Kapālabhāti type and three deep inspirations and expirations of the Ujjāyī type, speaking roughly. These very inspirations and expirations can again be arranged in four rounds: three rounds of Kapālabhāti of eleven expulsions each and one round of Ujjāyī of three breaths each. Now our experience has taught us that the three rounds of Bhastrikā put a greater strain on the system than the three rounds of Kapālabhāti and one round of Ujjāyī put together. This statement may not appeal to one who examines these exercises on smaller scale, but when they are compared on a larger scale the truth of it becomes at once evident.

Further our readers may recall what has been stated in the last but one paragraph of the preceding chapter. There we have said that as a breathing exercise Kapālabhāti is less harmful than Ujjāyī. But if Kapālabhāti is less innocent than Ujjāyī, Bhastrikā is much less innocent that way. Hence we should strongly advise a beginner first to start with lessons in Ujjāyī alone. When he has practised it a little and finds the same comfortable, he should add Kapālabhāti to his programme of the Yogic exercises. He might think of practising Bhastrikā, only when he becomes capable of taking up Kumbhaka. Here again we would advise a cautious arrangement. The three rounds of Kapālabhāti may give place to three rounds of Bhastrikā to begin with. Afterwards as the practice develops, the first part of Bhastrikā may be broken up into convenient groups of sixty, forty, thirty, and twenty each, every group being followed by the second part. Thus each round of Bhastrikā will be broken up into 2, 3, 4 and ultimately into six rounds. While laying down the measure of Kapālabhāti, we have recommended six rounds of it as the maximum for any physical culturist. Now if each round of Kapālabhāti is substituted by six rounds of Bhastrikā, the total number of Bhastrikā rounds amounts to thirty-six. We are sure this is more than sufficient for the needs of any student of physical culture.

When the rounds of Bhastrikā in the daily scheme of exercises exceed nine, it is desirable that the rounds of Ujjāyī are proportionately lessened. And when the maximum of thirty six rounds is attained in Bhastrikā, Ujjāyī is dropped altogether.[20]

The needs of a spiritual culturist are always greater than those of a physical culturist, so far as the Yogic exercises of spiritual value are concerned. Bhastrikā is emphatically an exercise of that nature. Hence Yogic students of spiritual culture required a larger measure of Bhastrikā than the one that is recommeded above.

In discussing the spiritual measure of Kapālabhāti, we have advised three rounds of three minutes each. Now when a spiritual student takes to Bhastrikā, he should progrssively break up these three rounds into six rounds each, so that the total number of Bhastrikā rounds would be eighteen at a sitting. If the student stands in need of a large dose of Bhastrikā for the day, he should add to these rounds or should have a larger number of sitting in the day. In arranging for this extra dose of Bhastrikā, students should never fail to consult an expert whom they may have chosen as their guide.

Out of the eight varieties of Prāṇāyāma, Bhastrikā has been mentioned as peculiarly capable of rousing the spiritual force. The Prāṇāyāma best prepares the mind for Pratyāhāra, Dhāraṇā, etc. It is wonderful exercise for lifting the individual above his flesh, and for bringing him to stand face to face with the serene spiritual

---

20. What has been said in this and the preceding pragraphs is intended to give the readers a general idea regarding the adjustment of breathing exercises. It is not meant to lay down any hard and fast rules. It may be pointed out here again, that Bhastrikā with twenty expirations is recommended by the author of *Gheraṇḍa-Saṃhita*.

light. Practise Bhastrikā religiously for a few months and the ecstatic joys of a Yogin are yours. Do not allow your enthusiasm to get the better of your reason, however, ever remembering the cautions pronounced at the end of the last two chapters.

CHAPTER VII

SŪRYABHEDANA

आसने सुखदे योगी बद्ध्वा चैवासनं ततः ।
दक्षनाड्या समाकृष्य बहिःस्थं पवनं शनैः ।। **H. P. II-48**
आ केशाद् आनखाग्रात् च्च निरोधावधि कुंभयेत् ।
ततः शनैः सव्यनाड्या रेचयेत् शनैः ।। **H. P. II-49**
पुनः पुनरिदं कार्य सूर्यभेदनमुत्तमम् ।। **H. P. II-50**

(āsane sukhade yogī baddhvā caivāsanaṃ tataḥ/
dakṣanāḍyā samākrṣya bahiḥsthaṃ pavanaṃ śanaiḥ)
(ā keśād a nakhāgrāt ca nirodhāvadhi kumbhayet/
tataḥ śanaiḥ savyanāḍya recayet pavanaṃ śanaiḥ)
(Punaḥ punaridaṃ kāryaṃ sūryabhednamuttama)

Translation

On a comfortable seat the Yogin should firmly take a Yoga pose, and then slowly breathing in the external air through the right nostril hold his breath, till he feels the pressure upto the hair (on his body) and upto the tips of his nails. Thereafter he should slowly breathe out though the left nostril. This excellent (Prāṇāyāma) Sūryabhedana should be repeated several times.

The Name

In Haṭha-Yoga literature Sūrya means the right and Candra means the left. For instance Sūryāṅga means the right side of the body whereas Candrāṅga means the left side as in H.P. III -15. So also Sūryanāḍī means either the right nostril or the right part of the nervous system and Candranāḍī means the opposite of them.

So in the verses under discussion Dakṣanāḍī signifies the right nostril and Savyanāḍī shows left nostril. In the name of the Prāṇāyāma itself the word Sūrya alone is used, although it stands for Dakṣanāḍī or Suryanāḍī. This is not unusual. We find in H.P. II-8, the word Sūrya alone is used for the right nostril and Candra for the left 'प्राणं सूर्येण च आकृष्य ... ... पुनः चन्द्रेण रेचयेत्' (prāṇāyāma sūryeṇa ca ākṛṣya punaḥ candreṇa recayet). Having inhaled air through the right nostril, one should exhale it again through the left nostril.

As will be seen later on in this particular Prāṇāyāma *along*, out of the eight varieties given by Svātmārma, inhalation through the right nostril is prescribed. No doubt in Bhastrikā also the same type of inhalation is laid down but the result of Bhastrikā is attributed to the combination of its two arts namely the Kapālabhāti part and the proper Prāṇāyāma part, whereas here the result is assigned to Prāṇāyāma alone. The result in both the cases is the awakening of Kuṇḍalinī and its passage through the six Cakras and three Granthis. Bhedana means opening out of blooming. The aim of all types of Prāṇāyāma is to wake up the dormant Kuṇḍalinī although this is not specifically mentioned in the case of Sūryabhedana.

So Sūryabhedana means that Prāṇāyāma which is used for the awakening of Kuṇḍalinī and in which inhalation is made through the right nostril.

Gheraṇḍa-Saṃhitā gives another explanation of the name of this Prāṇāyāma. After describing the technique of Sūryabhedana in V-57, 58, and mentioning the ten vital airs with their fields of activity from V- 59 to 64, the text says, 'सर्वे ते सूर्यसंभिन्नाः नाभिमूलात्

समुद्धरेत्' (sarve te sūryasaṃbhinnāḥ nābhimūlāt samuddharet). Here 'सूर्वे ते' stands for vital airs such as Prāṇa, Apāna etc., and 'सूर्य' stands for the air inhaled through the right nostril. 'संभिन्न' means combined. What Gheraṇḍa wants to say is that the air inhaled through the right nostril gets combined during Kumbhaka with all the ten vital airs that are functioning in the body. These combined airs accumulate at the root naval and are to be driven up 'समुद्धरेत्' (through suṣumṇa) from that root of the naval 'नाभिमूलात्'.

Here we are not going to discuss the technique of 'सूर्यभेदन्' as it is given by Gheraṇḍa. We have referred to Gheraṇḍa only to give another explanation of the name of this Prāṇāyāma. So according to *Gheraṇḍa-saṃhitā this* Prāṇāyāma is called 'सूर्यभेदन्' because in it the air inhaled through the right nostril gets combined with the ten vital airs in the body. Here it is easy to grasp what Gheraṇḍa wants to say but it is difficult to understand how 'भेद'or 'भेदन्' could be interpreted as.

The Technique

First of all the student of Yoga should arrange or a comfortable seat which he can continue to sit for a long time without any uneven pressure on his folded legs and hips which might cause discomfort. Then he should assume any meditative pose such as Padmāsana or Siddhāsana to which he may accustomed. When he is thus seated, he should slowly inhale external air through the right nostril and retain it till he feels the pressure all over his body right upto the hair and upto the end of his nails.[1] Here it is to be noted that

1. A reference to *Yoga-Mimāṃsā*, VI-55 would be desirable.

the student should consult his own capacity to begin with to develop his kumbhaka gradually step by step. Haste in this respect is likely to damage the lungs and may lead even to some incurable diseases. The Samskrta text does not mention here the formation of the three Bandhas, as they are common to all the types of Prāṇāyāma and have been stated in H.P. II-45 and 46. But we could strongly advise the students of Yoga to practise their Prāṇāyāma only with Jālandhara Bandh and avoid Uḍḍiyana and Mūla at least in the first stages of Abhyāsa. Even afterwards the full practice of Bandhas should be undertaken only under the guidance of a competent master. Jālandhara is particularly prescribed in this Prāṇāyāma, in *Gheraṇḍda-Saṃhitā,* V-58.

After holding the breath to capacity, the inhaled air is to be exhaled through the left nostril much more slowly than at the rate followed at the time of inhalation.

Pūraka, Kumbhaka and Recaka will form one round of Sūryabhedana. These rounds are to be repeated successively at one sitting according to the capacity of the individual. The questions of the manipulation of the nostrils, the time to be given respectively to Pūraka, Kumbhaka and Recaka etc., have been discussed at the relevant places.

1) **Pūraka** - (Inhale with Right Nostril)
2) **Kumbhaka** - (Pause with bandhas)
3) **Rechaka** - (Exhale with Left Nostril in double time)

CHAPTER VIII

ŚĪTKĀRĪ

सीत्कां तुर्यात तथा वक्त्रे घ्राणेनैव विजृंभिकाम् । H.P. II-53

(sītkāṃ kuryāt tathā vaktre ghrāṇenaiva vijṛmbhikām).

Translation

THROUGH the mouth the sound 'Sīt' should be produced (at the time of Pūraka). So also Recaka should be practised only through nose.

The Name

'सीत्कार' is the nominative singular of the word 'सीत्कारिन्' qualifying the masculine noun 'प्राणायाम'. 'सीत्कारिन्' means having or possessing the sound 'सीत्'. The word 'कार' is compounded with another word denoting a particular sound. So 'आकार' would mean the sound 'आ', 'मकार' would mean the sound, 'म', so on and so forth. In the same way 'सीत्कार' means the sound 'सीत्' and 'सीत्कारी' means that Prāṇāyāma in which the sound 'सीत्' is produced. Here we have to note that this sound is produced only in Pūraka and there too throughout inhalation only the sound 'सी' is produced and comes only at the end of the inhalation when the lips reclosed for Kumbhaka. So 'सीत्कारी' is an onomatopoetic word.

The Technique

First of all we have to note that the technique as it is described in the original text is not only concise but also incomplete. There is no reference to Kumbhaka. But as the author of H.P. has included

'सीत्कारी' in the eight Kumbhakas enumerated in H.P.., II- 44, the omission does not matter and we have to follow the general technique of Kumbhakas even in Sītkarī. The method of 'रेचक' is particularly stated as the exhalation is to be effected through both the nostrils and not through one only as in 'सूर्यभेदन' or 'भस्त्रिका'.

The peculiarity of this Prāṇāyāma lies in the method of its Pūraka. This method requires to be studied carefully with reference to the anatomy of the mouth and with the help of Fig. 43. The

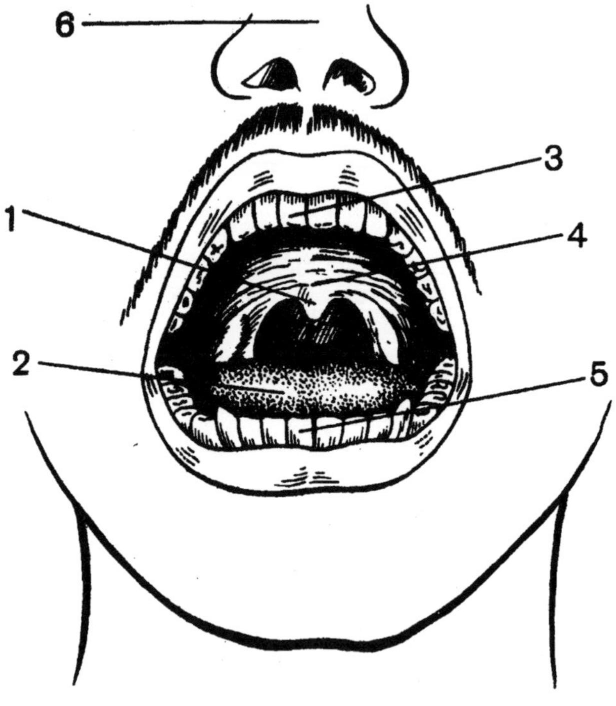

FIG. 43. The Mouth Widely Opened
(1) The Uvula (2) The Tongue (3) The Upper Set of Teeth
(4) The Soft Palate (5) The Lower Set of Teeth (6) The Nose

anatomical study of the mouth will become much more easy, if the student takes the help of a mirror. He should open his mouth wide as in Fig. 43 and stand facing light. The mirror should not be held exactly in front of the face but slightly on the right side so that the reflected light might fall inside the opened mouth. The lower set of teeth can be easily seen in the mirror while the mouth is wide open. But for observing the upper set of teeth the student will have to move his lower jaw a little upward and also draw up his upper lip a little. When this is done the upper teeth also will show themselves clearly.

Now it will be found that there are generally speaking in all 32 teeth, 16 the lower jaw and another 16 in the upper jaw corresponding to the former. Both these sets of 16 are to be divided into two parts each, thus forming four parts each consisting of eight teeth. Two parts on the right and two on the left. It will be clear that there is obvious correspondence in all these four parts.

Let us study the left set of teeth in the lower jaw. Just at the back end there are three very big teeth with two others following in their row which are big enough although smaller in mass. These five teeth we use for grinding our food. So the first three are called molars and the next two are called premolars. Next to these five there is one pointed tooth. It is called canine because it resembles a corresponding tooth in a dog. Following the canine tooth there are two teeth with rather sharp upper edges. As they are useful in cutting they are called incisors. A similar arrangement is to be found in all the remaining three sets.

Having studied the teeth arrangement it will be found easy to follow the technique of Pūraka in Sītkārī which is its peculiarity.

For this the student has to open his mouth a little by a slightly lowering the lower jaw and raising his upper lip a little. Then he has to put his tongue a bit beyond his lower incisors and then drawing its tip inside he is to press it against the incisor teeth. When this is done he will find the two borders of his tongue covering lower molars and premolars. He is then to raise the lower jaw so that the tongue is lightly pressed between upper and lower incisors. It is through this opening the air is to be sucked up in Pūraka producing the 'Sī' sound. The sound becomes the more pronounced because of moisture on the tongue.

When Pūraka is completed the tongue is withdrawn to its normal position in the mouth and the lips are closed. This closure of the lips produces the sound 'त्' and thus the whole sound of 'सीत्' is completed.

After usual Kumbhaka, Recaka begins through both the nostrils. When this is finished another round of 'सीत्कारी' follows, the number of such rounds being limited by the capacity of the student.

1) **Pūraka** - (Touch tip of the tounge to the front teeth Inhale through the mouth with See Sound)
2) **Kumbhaka** - (Pause with bandhas)
3) **Rechaka** - (Exhale with the both Nostril in double time)

CHAPTER IX

ŚĪTALĪ

जिह्वया वायुमाकृष्य पूर्ववत् कुंभसाधनम् ।
शनकैः घ्राणरंध्रायांम् रेचयेत् पवनं सुधीः ।। H.P. II-56.
........शीतली नाम कुंभिकेयम् ।। H.P. II-57.

(jthvayā vāyumākṛṣya pūvavat kumbhasādhanam
śanakaiḥ ghrāṇarandhrābhyām recayet pavanaṃ sudhiḥ)
.... śītalī nāma kumbhikeyam)

Translation

HAVING inhaled air though the tongue and having performed Kumbhaka as before (as in Sūryabhedana), an intelligent (student) should slowly exhale the air through both the nostrils. This Prāṇāyāma is called Śītalī.

The Name

The name of this Prāṇāyāma is derived from its cooling effect on the body. 'कुंभिका' is a feminine form of 'कुंभक' and 'शीतली' is the feminine form of 'शीतल' meaning cool and qualifies 'कुंभिका'.

The Technique

The lines from H.P. quoted above do not explain the whole technique. But the tradition is very clear in this regard and the commentary jyotsnā leaves us in no doubt, so also Śiva Saṃhitā, III-84 quoted at the end here.

The practice of this Prāṇāyāma starts with putting forth the tongue about 3/4 of an inch outside the lips. When this is done the tongue is to be folded double lengthwise, both inside and outside the mouth, so as to form a sort of a channel almost making a tubelike formation below the upper lip. The outer end of the tongue will naturally form a narrower channel sloping towards the tip of the tongue. When thus arranged the tongue assumes the form of the lower part of a bird's beak (Fig. 42). This lingual channel is to be used for inhaling air from outside at the time Pūraka. Inhalation over, the tongue is to withdrawn and lips are to be closed.

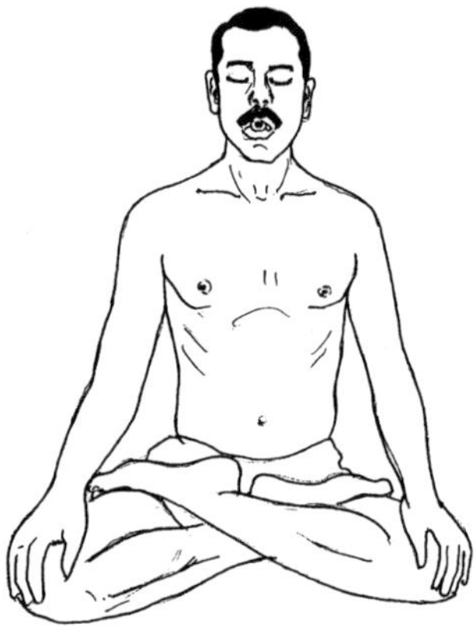

FIG. 42. The Tongue Arranged as a Bird's Beak.

Kumbhaka is of the usual type. Recaka is to be performed slowly as in other cases, but through both the nostrils at the same time.

In explaining the name of this Prāṇāyāma we have stated that it is due to the cooling effect of it on the body. This effect is due to the air being sucked up through the mouth and not through the nose. Physiologically the nose is intended not only for breathing but also for warming up the external cool air before it enters the lungs. What is taken for granted in this Prāṇāyāma is that the external air is neither above body temperature nor far below it. Hotter air will fail to give the cooling effect. If the air is far below the body temperature it may affect the lungs adversely. Śītalī is to be practised in hot season inside a cool cell in an Āsrama. Śiva Saṃhitā, actually speaks of inhaling cool air.

III-84. (kākacañcvā pibet vāyuṃ Śītalam). Kākacañcu is the tongue folded like a crow's beak.

1) **Pūraka** - (Bring your tounge 3/4 of an inche out side the lower lip assume the form of bird's beak, Inhale through tube like formation)
2) **Kumbhaka** - (Pause with bandhas)
3) **Rechaka** - (Exhale with the both Nostril in double time)

CHAPTER X

BHRĀMARĪ

वेगाद् घाषं पूरकं भृङ्गनादम् ।
भृङ्गीनादं रेचकं मन्दमन्दम् ।।
योगीन्द्राणामेवमभ्यासयोगात् ।
चित्ते जाता काचिदानन्दलीला ।। **H.P. II - 67**

(vegād ghoṣaṃ pūrakaṃ bhṛṅganādam/
bhṛṅgīnādaṃ recakaṃ mandamandam/
yogīindrāṇām evemabhyāsayogāt/
citte jātā kācidānandalīlā)

Translation

BY quick forced inspiration one should produce a high humming sound like that of a male bee and by very slow expiration a low sound should be produced resembling that of a female bee. By a continuous practice of this type there easily supervenes a condition of bliss in the minds of eminent Yogins that defies all description.

The Name

'भ्रामरी' is the feminine form of 'भ्रामर' which is an adjective derived from 'भ्रमरी' meaning a bee. 'भ्रामरी' qualifies 'कुंभिका' which is to be supplied. In fact the whole verse does not make any reference to Kumbhaka which is to be understood from H. P. II-44 which includes 'भ्रामरी' in the list of Kumbhakas to be described thereafter. This Kumbhaka is called 'भ्रामरी' because its technique requires the production of a sound resembling that of a bee both in Pūraka and Recaka.

The Technique

From the name of the Kumbhaka we find that its Pūraka and Recaka require the production of a high and low humming sound respectively. So we have to understand how this humming sound is to be produced.

We often find persons snoring in their sleep. That snoring is rough and irregular. Besides, it occurs only during inhalation. But if the snoring could be made voluntary, smooth and prolonged and also could be effected during exhalation, the sounds will roughly resemble those of a male and female bee required in Pūraka and Recaka respectively.

But how docs a man snore ? The explanation is easy to understand. If we refer to Fig. 43, we find that the posterior part of the palate is soft. It forms the soft palate to which the small organ uvula is attached. The edges of this soft palate are very thin and are capable of vibrating if they are made to obstruct a current of air. In ordinary smooth breathing, whether in a waking or in a sleeping condition, the air inhaled through the nose glides gently across the soft palate and there is noice produced. The same is the case when the man breathes out. But in snoring the soft palate gets lifted up, and approaching the wall of the pharynx behind (Fig. 3), partially obstructs the passage of air breathed in. The thin edges of the soft palate then start vibrating and produce the snoring sound. In some persons this obstruction is caused even in exhalation. But in that case most of the air escapes through the mouth and there are no vibrations of the soft palate as in the case of inhalation. In inspiration air is being sucked up by the lungs to get the oxygen that is needed by the body but in expiration air is to be driven out to get rid of CO_2. So it may escape through the nose but it may also escape through the mouth without any physiological disadvantage. Anyway, we understand now how a man snores.

But there are people whose snoring involves even nasal sounds of various types, the nature of these sounds depending upon the nasal part which the air strikes in inhalation. In understanding 'भ्रामरी' we have to take into consideration not only snoring as such but also these nasal sounds. The only nasal sound occurring in 'भ्रामरी' is the sound of 'N' in the pronounciation of the word *king.*

If we have caught this nasal sound and understood how a man snores, we can easily follow the technique of 'भ्रामरी'.

Try to imitate snoring and observe mentally the movement of the soft palate (Fig.3). It will be found that the soft palate is lifted and drawn towards the nasal part of the pharynx (Fig. 3.). This movement can actually be left inside the mouth. Then draw the soft palate still closer to the pharynx, and inhale. A beautiful sound produced by a combination of gentle vibrations of the soft palate and the nasal friction will be heard. In the beginning this is rather rough and irregular but by practice it can be made so sweet and sonorous that the listener may feel as if a string instrument is being played upon by some dexterous musician. This much for Pūraka.

Kumbhaka is of the usual type and does not require any explanation. 'रेचक' requires the same movement of the soft palate. Very often students of Yoga think that if they produce a nasal only, it would give 'भ्रामरी रेचक'. But that idea is mistaken. Nasal sound can be produced even without the vibration of the soft palate. But 'भ्रामरी' requires not only the nasal sound but also the action of the soft palate. So even in Recaka one has to lift the soft palate, just as in Pūraka and with the air that is being exhaled produce the nasal sound and the vibrations of the soft palate.

Now 'रेचक' ordinarily is to take double the time given to 'पूरक'. Hence the flow of air striking the edges of the soft palate and nasal passage will be slower and the sound produced will be gentler in comparison to the Pūraka sound. It will be lower in pitch.

Even in the case of a beginner the music of 'भ्रामरी' is so enchanting that the mind gets deeply absorbed in it and pleasurable sensations are felt all over the body and mind. It is, then, no wonder that 'भ्रामरी' performed to excellence by Yogins who have reached the sublime heights of perfection should lead them to indescribable bliss.

Ghreaṇḍa-Saṃhitā in V-77 to 88 gives another technique and *Śiva Saṃhitā* in V-39 to 48 describes still another under the name of Rāja Yoga.

1) **Pūraka** - (Inhale with both Nostril producing sound of bee)
2) **Kumbhaka** - (Pause with bandhas)
3) **Rechaka** - (Exhale with the both Nostril producing sound of bee, gentle and lowpitch sound in comparison to Puraka)

CHAPTER XI

MŪRCCHĀ

पूरकान्ते गाढतरं बद्ध्वा जालंधरं शनैः ।
रेचयेत् मूर्च्छनाख्येयं मनोमूर्च्छा सुखप्रदा ।। **H.P. II - 68**

(pūrakānte gāḍhataraṃ baddhvā jālandharaṃ śanaiḥ/
recayet mūrcchanākhyeyaṃ manomurcchā sukhapradā).

Translation

AT the end of Pūraka one should very firmly form Jālandhara (chin-lock) and then slowly exhale. This (Prāṇāyma) is called Mūrcchanā. It leads to loss of awareness and is pleasant.

The Name

When we study the physiology of the technique of this Kumbhaka, we will be able to understand how that technique is capable of bringing about loss of awareness. In Haṭha Yoga this loss of awareness is said to have some spiritual value being an aid to meditation. In fact in some traditions this loss of awareness is brought about by administration of some drugs along with the practice of Prāṇāyāma. For instance in L. Y. V. XXVIII-122 we have the following:

प्राणायामदृढाभ्यासैः युक्त्या च गुरुदत्तया ।
आसनाशनयोगेन प्राणस्पन्दो निरुध्यते ।।

(Prāṇāyāmadṛḍhabhyasaiḥ yuktyā ca gurudttayā/
āsanāśanayogena prāṇaspando nirudhyate).

Mūrcchā

What this verse means is this. The movement of breath is arrested by means of well established practice of Prāṇāyāma, some skilful knack shown by the guide and the proper use of Yoga postures and diet.

Now Vi. Nya. commenting in this verse in his Ji. Mu. Vi. explains some of these tricks and among them mentions 'विस्मृतिप्रदौषधिसेवा' (vismṛtipradauṣadhisevā) i.e., taking some drug which is capable of bringing about loss of awareness.

H.P. possibly wants to combine the effects of Prāṇāyāma and 'विस्मृतिप्रदौषधिसेवा' in one and the same practice and develops the technique given here. That is why this Kumbhaka is called 'मूर्च्छा' which means loss of awareness.

The Technique

At the end of deep inhalation one is to practise Kumbhaka with Jālandhara as in other types of Prāṇāyāma. But in this case Jālandhara is to be so tightly fixed and is to be maintained so long as would lead to a sort of stupor. How Jālandhara is capable of inducing stupor is explained in the note on this Bandha given at the beginning of this part. Another point in the technique of this Prāṇāyāma which is peculiar to it is the continuation of Jālandhara even during Recaka. Elsewhere Jālandhara is required to be released at the end of Kumbhaka.

No doubt a single round of 'मूर्च्छा' will not cause stupor. But when a large number of rounds is undertaken at every sitting and the practice is continued from day to day, it will led to a mental condition which amounts to loss of awareness. This condition of mind is said by Haṭha-Yogins to be not only pleasant but also helpful in concentration as it excludes all sensory disturbances and leaves the mind free from associating ideas.

Gheraṇḍa-Saṃhitā V-83 gives different technique of this Prāṇāyāma where it prescribes mind to be fixed between the two eye-brows.

CHAPTER XII

PLĀVINĪ

अन्तःप्रवर्तितोदारमारुतापूरितोदरः ।
पयस्यगाधेऽपि सुखात् प्लवते पद्मपत्रवत् ।। H.P. II - 69

(antaḥpravartitodāramārutāpūritodaraḥ
payasyagādhe api sukhāt plavate padmapatravat)

Translation

WITH the stomach completely filled up with liberal quantity of air introduced (through the oesophagus) and with the lungs similarly filled up (through the wind-pipe) a Yogin easily floats like a lotus leaf even on deepest waters.

The Name

The adjective 'प्लाविनी' qualifies the feminine noun 'कुंभिका' and is itself used here as a noun. The root from which it is derived is 'प्लु' (meaning 'to float') in its causal form. So 'प्लाविनी' means a Prāṇāyāma that enables a man to float.

Even ordinarily a man can float on water easily, provided he throws back his head and dips it a little in water. This is because of the buoyancy of water and the low specific gravity of human body. Then the question arises as to what is the special efficiency of this Prāṇāyāma on account of which it should get the name of Plāvinī. The answer is that this Kumbhaka lowers the specific gravity much more below the normal, so much so that the human body remains almost on the surface of water like a lotus leaf. It is well known that in ordinary floating a part of the man's body sinks below the water surface but in Plāvinī it does not. Hence the propriety of the name. How the specific gravity is lowered will be clear presently when we study the technique of this Kumbhaka.

The Technique

This Prāṇāyāma requires air to be introduced into the stomach and also into the lungs. The introduction of air into the lungs is a normal affair. In Prāṇāyāmas one has to make this inhalation as deep as possible. So there is nothing unusual in it. But pumping air into the stomach is neither natural nor usual. But a student of Plāvinī has first to fill his stomach completely before he is to start his Pūraka. We now want to see how this is done.

When we eat food or drink water we first take it into our mouth and then swallow it through the oesophagus (Fig. 3). Now at the lower end of the oesophagus there is a muscular ring called the cardiac sphincter which ordinarily remains closed, but which opens automatically for food or water that is swallowed and that food or water finds its way into the stomach. The student of Plāvinī is to imitate this action (swallowing) with air. He first takes mouthful of it and then closing his mouth ties to swallow it. Some saliva gets mixed with this air and when swallowing is imitated the air with the saliva goes down the oesophagus and finds its way to the stomach through the cardiac sphincter. By practice this eating of air becomes so easy that one can get his stomach inflated enormously with the result that the abdomen bulges out and its muscles become so much stretched that a little tapping gives out a sonorous sound ! This air can remain in the stomach for a long time and by practice can be driven out through the oesophagus and the mouth artificially, just as it comes out in eructations.. An expert can take out very large quantities of the swallowed air in a continuous stream of air and empty the stomach completely in two or three attempts !

Thus far the Yogin has dealt with his stomach only. But after filling it completely he deals with his lungs and practises his deepest Pūraka and Kumbhaka. After retaining his breath as long as he could, he practises Recaka, all the while keeping his stomach inflated with air that he has swallowed in the beginning. After putting in the desired number of rounds of Prāṇāyāma he empties his stomach also.

The large quantities of air introduced in the stomach and the lungs increase remarkably the size of the abdomen and the chest and air being far lighter than water, the specific gravity of the Yogin is lowered enabling him to float almost on the surface of water. This does not, however, mean that Plāvinī is to be practised while floating. Nay, it is performed as other Prāṇāyāmas in a sitting position on a comfortable set. The name Plāvinī is given only to denote the special feature of this Kumbhaka.

CHAPTER XIII

PHYSIOLOGICAL AND SPIRITUAL VALUES OF PRĀṆĀYĀMA[1]

In Chapter I, we studied the physiology of normal respiration. In the second we noticed the different poses etc., an individual has to assume, when he tries to educate his respiratory system through Prāṇāyāmic exercises, with a view to attaining physical or spiritual excellence. In chapter III we passed under rapid survey some of the most salient features of Prāṇāyāma in general, particularly Prāṇāyāmas, namely, Ujjāyī and Bhastrikā being studied in some detail in the next three chapters. In this last chapter of the present handbook, we wish to evaluate Prāṇāyāma from the physiological and spiritual points of view. First we shall ascertain its physiological value and then the spiritual.

The physiological value of an exercise depends upon its capacity to confer health upon the person practising it. The greater the degree of health an exercise is calculated to induce, the more

---

1. We have tried to write this chapter in as popular a language as the subject allowed it. We have not, however, sacrificed scientific accuracy. But as a result of our attempt to make things simple many statements have remained scientifically incomplete. To give one example out of many. In our discussion about the organs of elimination we have made no reference to the skin which is, perhaps, as important as the other three organs which have been mentioned therein. Our readers are, therefore, requested not to expect scientific completeness in this chapter, but should turn to *Yoga- Mimāṃsā* for satisfying their desire for thoroughness.

valuable it will be, But what is health ? Health may be defined as the harmonious functioning of the different systems working in the human body. The principal systems are the nervous, the endocrine, the respiratory, the circulatory and the digestive. Out of these the nervous and the endocrine are of supreme importunace, but even they have to depend upon the other systems enumerated above. We shall now proceed to see in what way and to what degree, Prāṇāyāma is able to influence these systems and secure their efficient and harmonious working. But before we do this we shall briefly notice the functions of the different systems which we are going to examine.

Starting with the study of the nervous system, we many compare it to a big power house generating electricity and a network of wires that distributes it to the different machines in a factory. The brain, the spinal cord and the sympathetic cords constitute the power house. The nerves starting from the brain, or from the spinal cord, represent the electric wires in the factory of human body. In a regular factory every piece of machinery is set in motion by the electric current carried to it across the wires from the power house. Similarly, in the factory of human body all physical movements depend upon the impulses carried across the nerves from the brain and the cords. Let the power house go out of order or let there be obstruction in the current of electricity flowing across the wires, the whole machinery will come to a standstill. Similarly, if the brain and the cords are damaged, or the nerves are so degenerated as not to convey the impulses, physical movements will stop. The effects of this cessation of physical movements, have a deeper meaning than an ordinary reader can imagine. Our digestion, our blood circulation and even our respiration is controlled and carried on by the nervous impulses brought to the organs responsible for these functions, from the brain and the cords. In case the nervous impulses do not start or having started do not reach their destination, all life processes will stop, and even the spark of life may become extinct. Such is the supreme importance of the nervous system.

Now in the illustration of the power house taken in the previous paragraph, granting that the power house does generate electricity, and the wires do conduct that electricity to their terminals, but the current of electricity is not of sufficient strength, the machinery supplied by that electricity will not move. For the necessary movement, the electric current must be of the required strength. In the machinery of human body this strength of the current depends upon the secretions of what are called the *endocrine glands.* The whole nervous mechanism may be in perfect order, and yet if the endocrine secretions are not available in the necessary quantity and of the necessary quality, the strength of the nerve-impulse and the nerves themselves later on will degenerate. Consequently physical movements and the life processes will become dull and languid. Let us take one of these glands for illustration. Say the thyroid. This is the most popularly known endocrine gland, although the sex glands both in males and females, the pituitary body etc., are of no less importance. Remove the thyroid from a healthy person and his eyes begin to be pale, his cheeks begin to sink, his muscles begin to be flabby or lean, his hair begin to turn gray and he becomes a prey to premature old age. Restore the thyroid and the man begins to show all the sign of youthful enthusiasm. Symptoms of old age are gone, the person begins to walk erect, things brighten up and life again becomes a pleasure. Thus it will be seen that the endocrine system stands on the same level of physiological importance as the nervous system.

Study of human physiology clearly indicated that these two systems of infinite importance in the human organism, have to depend upon the circulatory system for getting the necessary blood supply and upon the respiratory and the digestive systems for getting the blood of the necessary quality. The circulatory system consists of the heart, the arteries, the veins and the capillaries. It is the duty of this system to take the blood to every tissue in the human body. The nerves and the endocrine glands, if they are starved for want of the necessary blood supply, will degenerate in their functions. The result will be what has been stated in the last two paragraphs.

It is, however, of no practical use to have the circulatory system in an efficient condition, if the quality of the blood that is being circulated through it is not rich. If the blood is loaded with toxins, the efficiency of the circulatory system will be of little consequence. So the quality of the blood must be kept rich, and for this human physiology has to depend upon the respiratory and the digestive systems.

In order that the blood may be rich in quality, it must carry the necessary quantity of oxygen with it and also contain elements of nutrition for the tissues. The blood gets oxygen from the air inhaled and the elements of nutrition from the absorption of food-stuffs and drinks. The quantity of oxygen the blood can carry, will mainly depend upon the efficiency of the respiratory system. With defective respiration the absorption of oxygen into the blood will be insufficient and the tissues supplied by the blood deficient in oxygen will be starved. So also one may use rich food-stuffs and luxuriant drinks, but if the digestive apparatus is not in order, there will be little digestion and absorption, and most of the stuff will be wasted, with the result that the blood will contain very small elements of nutrition. Thus we see that the respiratory and the digestive systems must work effectively if the blood supply is to be constantly kept rich in quality.

A defective working of the respiratory and digestive systems not only keeps the blood poorer in quality for want of oxygen and nutritive elements, but it loads the blood with waste matter which is poisonous. We shall explain this point further. Carbon dioxide is constantly manufactured in the body. The efficiently working circulatory system carries this poisonous gas to the lungs and then gets rid of it. But if the efficiency of this system suffers, this waste matter accumulates in the different tissues and there produces toxic effect. Similarly food-stuffs leave a very large wastage. It is for the bowels to throw it out. The smaller the degree of digestion and absorption of food and drink, the larger is the wastage. And if the bowels which are anatomically included in the digestive tube, do not work efficiently, this waste matter remains lodged in the colon or even in the small intestine for several days, giving rise to highly dangerous toxins. These toxins get into the current of the blood through the walls of the bowels and poison the blood and the poisonous blood being circulated throughout the body, leads to the degeneration of the whole organism.

We have seen in the previous paragraph how the lungs and the bowels act as organs of elimination. The kidneys are also organs of the same type. Some of the waste products which are poisonous in nature, are driven out of the human organism with the urine. If the kidneys do not function satisfactorily these poisonous substances are held back and find a resting place especially in the different joints of the human body. People suffering from gout have invariably defective kidneys. Thus it is clear that the blood in order to be rich in quality has to depend upon the respiratory and the digestive systems and in order to be free from toxic elements, it has to depend upon the organs of elimination.

Thus far we have studied some of the broadest features of the most important physiological systems upon the harmonious functioning of which, human health depends. We shall now proceed to examine how Prāṇāyāma helps the efficient functioning of these systems.

Starting with the organs of elimination, we find that the bowels and the kidneys are situated in the abdomen and the lungs in the chest. In normal respiration and alternate rise and fall of the diaphragm and the alternate contraction and relaxation of the abdominal muscles give constant movement and gentle massage to the bowels and the kidneys. During Prāṇāyāma in both inspiration and expiration well as in retention of breath, this movement and massage are greatly accentuated. If there be any congestion it is relieved because of the pressure exerted. The nerves and muscles which control the functions of the bowels and the kidneys are all toned up. Thus the bowels and the kidneys derive benefit not only during the time that Prāṇāyāma is being practised, but even for the remaining part of the day. The nerves and muscles once toned up continue to maintain that tone for a considerably long time. The bowels and the kidneys rendered healthier due to Prāṇāyāma carry on their functions of elimination more effectively.

The same is the case with the lungs. As we have seen in the first chapter healthy respiration depends upon strong respiratory muscles and good elasticity of the lungs. On the physical side Prāṇāyāma is a culture of these muscles and the lungs. By opening out the chest to its fullest extent several times a day and by putting the lungs on a stretch to the utmost possible extent, these organs are best educated to perform their functions satisfactorily. As in the case of bowels and kidneys so in the case of the lungs the training given to them for a short time, prepares them for efficient working during the remaining part of the day. Thus Prāṇāyāma is a very valuable exercise for the organs of elimination.

Organs of digestion and absorption do not stand on a different level so far as the effects of Prāṇāyāma on them are concerned. The stomach, the pancreas and the liver which play a very prominent part in the digestion of food and drink, are all exercised in Prāṇāyāma on account of the massage given to them by the diaphragm and the abdominal muscles. In a very large number of people who are dyspeptic and constipated, the liver becomes habitually congested and consequently faulty in function. For relieving this congestion Prāṇāyāma is an excellent exercise. An unhealthy pancreas gets very good stimulus and correction by Prāṇāyāmic exercises. In our clinical experience we have noticed a number of cases being effectively relieved of their gastric disorder, mainly as a result of Prāṇāyāma. With a perfectly functioning system, absorption also becomes perfect, and the blood is enriched with the necessary nutritive elements.

A liberal supply of oxygen to the circulating blood current, is of supreme importance for the heath of an individual. This supply is effectively improved by means of Prāṇāyāma. The scope of this handbook does not allow us to enter into physiological details. We refer our readers to the volumes of Yoga-Miṃāṃsā for evidence that conclusively proves the statements that we are presently going to make.

Prāṇāyāma performed according to the technique given in the preceding chapters of improving the oxygen supply of the blood as no other exercise is. This is not because during the process of Prāṇāyāma an individual absorbs a large quantity of oxygen, but because of the training of the respiratory system which helps the individual for twenty four hours. The impression that an individual absorbs larger quantities of oxygen in Prāṇāyāma is merely a superstition. We shall explain how. Any Prāṇāyāma worth the name should have every round of it to cover at least one minute. Now an average person inhales in one minute about 7,000 mi. of air during normal inspiration. The same individual during Prāṇāyāma will inhale at the most 3,700 ml. in one minute. The total intake of air being far smaller in Prāṇāyāma, the absorption of oxygen is consequently smaller. We have conclusively proved in Yoga-Miṃāṃsā on the strength of experimental evidence that the degree of absorption of oxygen does not vary in proportion to the time for which breath is retained. For this reason even when Breath is held even for half a minute, the increase in the absorption of oxygen over the normal absorption is not considerable. Thus it will be clear that the idea that an individual absorbs larger quantities of oxygen during Prāṇāyāma is myth.

Where then is the advantages of practising Prāṇāyāma for enriching the blood with oxygen ? The answer to this question is as follows. Even when temporarily during the process of Prāṇāyāma an individual absorbs smaller quantities of oxygen, the Prāṇāyāmic exercises so train the respiratory apparatus that during the remaining part of the day respiration is carried on most efficiently and larger quantities of oxygen are absorbed throughout the day, than they ordinarily would do.

In the chapter on Ujjāyi we have recommended the rate of four rounds of it in a minute. This recommendation is for people who practise only Recaka and Pūraka. For ordinary purposes of physical culture this is sufficient. It is to be noted that when four rounds of Ujjāyī are performed in a minute, the quantity of oxygen absorbed even during the Prāṇāyāmic process, is much larger than in ordinary respiration. Again the training of the respiratory apparatus by means of having four rounds of Ujjāyī in a minute, is sufficient for all practical purposes of physical culture.

With the efficient functioning of the organs of digestion, elimination and respiration, the quality of the blood remains satisfactory. Now this blood is to be distributed to the different tissues of the body. This is the duty of the circulatory system and especially of the heart. It has been admitted even by the Western scientists that practices in deep breathing give a gentle massage to the heart. We have carefully studied the pressure changes that are produced round about the heart in Prāṇāyāma. And we are happy to note that the technique of Prāṇāyāma as it is given in Yoga, establishes conditions much more favourable for this massage, than the condition secured in the Western type of deep breathing. For the elucidation of this point we again refer our readers to the volumes of Yoga-Mimāṃsā.[2] Now the heart which is the principal organ of circulation being made healthier by Prāṇāyāma, the whole circulatory system works satisfactorily.

But the matter does not end there. In Bhastrikā, especially in its part which corresponds to Kapālabhāti, vibrations start and spread themselves to nearly every tissue in the human organism, the arteries, the veins and the capillaries included. Thus the whole circulatory system is exercised and massaged during Prāṇāyāma and is prepared for efficient functioning.

Next we come to the nervous and the endocrine systems. The rich quality of the blood and its satisfactory distribution to all the nerves and glands ensure their health. During Prāṇāyāma especially during Bhastrikā, the circulation of the blood becomes very rapid and the quality of the blood is also rendered very rich. (Evidence on this point has already been collected in our laboratory). This richer and more liberal blood supply brought to the endocrine glands makes them healthier. The same is the case with the brain, the spinal cord, the cranial and the spinal nerves and the sympathetic.

The advantage derived from a richer and more liberal blood supply is not the only advantage the nervous system gets from

2. Vide 'Pressure Changes in Prāṇāyāma', Vol. IV, No. 1.

Prāṇāyāma. The nerves are directly exercised. During Pūraka the diaphragm is contracted and lowered and the abdominal muscles are kept controlled, that is, slightly contracted. The combined action of the diaphragm and the abdominal muscles pulls up the lower part of the spinal column. If Jālandhara Bandha is practised the upper part of the spinal column is also pulled up. This pulling up of the vertebral column as a whole, gives exercise to the sympathetic and the roots of the spinal nerves.

Limitations of this handbook do not allow us even to make a passing reference to the exercise of the brain by the Prāṇāyāma processes. Suffice it to say that the whole nervous system is very finely exercised by the practice of Prāṇāyāma. Thus the nervous and the systems which are of supreme importance in human physiology and also the respiratory, the circulatory and the digestive systems upon which the health of the first two systems depends, are all simultaneously exercised in Prāṇāyāma. Every round either of Ujjāyī or Bhastrikā makes the organism healthier. In fact the Yogic seers of ancient India looked upon Prāṇāyāma as the one exercise that could make every life process supremely healthy. Some of them were so enthusiastic in their optimism about the physiological efficacy of Prāṇāyāma that they ruled out all other exercises for securing health of human body. From our own experience we can safely say that no physical exercise can even have one hundredth of the efficacy of Prāṇāyāma. In fact Prāṇāyāma is not only the control of different physiological functions but it is the control of the very life processes that vitalize the human organism.

* * * * *

The spiritual value of Prāṇāyāma is equally great. People fail to understand how a physical process could lead to spiritual development. Today we do not have sufficient *laboratory* evidence to convince those that are prejudiced against Yoga. But we can surely offer a few remarks on this point which will appear to people who have an impartial but sympathetic attitude towards Yoga. Students of endocrinology are coming to the conclusion that the endocrine glands are capable of influencing not only the physiology but also the psychology of an individual. The most optimistic of them feel that they could change criminals into saints by means of treating endocrine glands. Personally we do not know how far this optimism is justifiable. In fact, orthodox scientists do not accept everything that endocrinology has to say. But even they cannot deny the fact that the endocrine glands materially influence the psychology of a person.

Hypothetically we are satisfied that particular nerve-centres have influence on human psychology similar to the influence of the glands of internal secretion. That these centres of the human nervous system could be effectively worked upon and made to experience extraordinary impulses and vibrations, is a fact of every day experience for practical students of Yoga. It is our fond hope that a day will arise when these impulses and vibrations could be demonstrated objectively in the laboratory of the *Kaivalyadhama* and their influence on human psychology could be scientifically established. The day may come when it will. Today we will explain how the different centres are worked upon through the physiology of Prāṇāyāma. As the scope of this handbook does not allow us to enter into details, we will give here merely a broad outline of our explanation.

First of all we have to note that the alveolar surface of the lungs presents by far the vastest area from which interoceptive impulses travel to the brain particularly when the lungs are stretched to their fullest extent. This area is not restricted to the lungs alone, but extends to the bronchioles, bronchi, trachea and the larynx. Thus even on neuro-anatomical grounds one could expect a possibility of an integration of the autonomic and cerebrospinal impulses which brings about a balanced condition of the mind and which raises consciousness to higher and higher planes.

Further in *Yoga-Mimāṃsā* we have discussed the intrathoracic and intra-pulmonic pressure changes in Prāṇāyāma. The intra-abdominal pressures also undergo considerable changes in Prāṇāyāmic exercises. It can be easily proved that all the three types of pressures referred to just now, are rendered extremely high during Prāṇyāma practised with the three Bandhas-Mūla, Uḍḍiyāna and Jālandhara. This high pressure gives peripheral stimulus to the different nerve plexuses situated in the abdomen and the thorax.

Again we are hypothetically satisfied that the practice of Prāṇāyāma introduces high pressures both in the central canal of the spinal cord and the ventricles of the brain. These pressures centrally stimulate the whole nervous system. Owing to these central and peripheral stimuli, the human consciousness begins to be internalized and supersensuous perceptions begin to be possible. Worlds subtler and still subtler begin to be opened out in proportion to the consciousness itself getting more and more refined, till at last the individual consciousness merges into the cosmic and the individual becomes one with the Infinite.

APPENDIX-I

A FULL COURSE IN YOGIC PHYSICAL CULTURE

For an average man of health

ĀSANAS

1.	Śīrṣāsana	...	1/4 min. to 12 mins., adding 1/2 min per week.
2.	Sarvāṅgāsana	...	1/2 min. to 6 mins., adding 1 min. per week.
3.	Matsyāsana	...	1/4 min. to 3 mins., adding 1/4 min. per week.
4.	Halāsana	...	1 min. to 4 mins., for all stages put together, adding 1 min. per week
5.	Bhujaṅgāsana	...	3 to 7 turns each, the pose being maintained for 10 secs., adding one turn every fortnight to each.
6.	Śalabhāsana		
7.	Dhanurāsana		
8.	Ardha-Matsyendrāsana	...	1/4 min. to 1 min., for each side, adding 1/4 min. per week
9.	Paścimatāna	...	1/4 min. to 1 min., adding 1/4 min. per week.
10.	Mayūrāsana	...	1/6 min. or 10 secs. to 2 mins., adding 1/4 min. per week.
11.	Śavāsana	...	2 mins. to 10 mins., adding 2 mins. per week

BANDHA

1. Uḍḍiyāna ... 3 to 7 turns, adding 1 turn per week.

MUDRĀ

1. Yoga-Mudrā ... 1 min. to 3 mins., adding 1 min. per week.

KRIYĀS

1. Nauli ... 3 to 7 turns, adding 1 turn per week
2. Kapālabhāti ... 3 rounds of 11 to 121 expulsions each, adding 11 expulsions to each round every week.

PRĀṆĀYĀMAS

1. Ujjāyi ... 7 to 28 rounds, adding 3 rounds every week.
2. Bhastrikā ... 3 rounds of 11 to 121 expulsions each, adding 11 expulsions to each round every round week. Every round to be followed by a suitable Kumbhaka.

A FEW HINTS REGARDING THE FULL COURSE

Limitations

1. Students of Yogic Physical Culture will do well to remember the limitations that have been indicated from time to time in Yoga- Miṃāṃsā for each exercise; and which have been summarized here in the following section.

2. People suffering from running ears, weak eye capillaries, and

weak heart should avoid the practice of Śīrṣāsana. This, Viparīta Karaṇī and Sarvāṅgāsana may be very cautiously practised by those that are troubled by chronic nasal catarrh. Bhujaṅgāsana, Śalabhāsana and Dhanurāsana are to be avoided by persons with considerable tenderness in the abdominal viscera, especially when the spleen is excessively enlarged. Constipated people with be well advised not to practise Yoga Mudrā and Paścimatāna on a large measure. Generally speaking weakness in the heart should exclude the exercises of Uḍḍiyāna, Nauli, Bhastrikā and Kapālabhāti. Weakness of the lungs also indicates the exclusion of Kapālabhāti as well as Bhastrikā and Ujjāyi Kumbhakas, although the Recaka and Pūraka of Ujjāyi are available even to people with weak lungs. Persons recording blood pressure above 150 and below 100 mm. Hg. habitually, should exclude the Yogic exercises altogether, provided they are going to undertake these exercises on their own responsibility.

N.B. - Anyone suffering from considerable weakness in any part of the body will do well to consult an expert for giving him the necessary exercises.

Measures

3. The course is perfectly general. The proportion of time shown against each exercise is also general and has no reference to individual cases.

4. Students may stop short with only half the maximum time put down for each exercise, provided that they observe the relative proportion among the different practices.

5. In section 6 another alternative is shown.
6. The maximum to be reached in the different exercises in the FULL COURSE, may also be as follows : Śīrṣāsana, 6 mins.; Sarvāñgāsana, 3 mins.; Matsyāsana, 1 min.; Halāsana, 2 mins.; Bhujañgāsana, Śalabhāsana and Dhanurāsana, 3 mins. each; Ardha-Matsyendrāsana, Paścimatāna and Mayūrāsana, 1 min. each; Uḍḍiyāna, 2 mins.; Yoga-Mudrā, 1 min.; Nauli, 3 mins.; Kapālabhāti of Bhastrikā, 8 mins. and Ujjāyi, 7 mins.
7. People who want to reduce their time of exercise to the lowest possible minimum, should take up the SHORT COURSE.

Caution

8. Under no circumstances should the exercises lead to languor. The student should come out of his practices fully refreshed, a sort of quiet settling over his nerves.
9. The whole course need not be gone through at a stretch. It may be profitable punctuated with convenient periods of rest.
10. Even then care should be taken to see that the total amount of energy expended does not strain the system.
11. *Be with caution bold* is our repeated advice to the student of Yogic Physical Culture.
12. If there is a considerable break in the practice of these exercises, whenever the exercises are to be started again, they should start on a humbler scale, although the full measure may be reached somewhat rapidly.
13. After severe illness the Yogic exercises should be undertaken only when the patient recovers sufficient energy for their

practice. It would always be desirable, by way of a cautious measure, to prefix to the practice of these exercises, a moderately long walk everybody for a week or so.

14. Yogic exercises should never commence for an hour and a half after even a moderate quantity of solid food or a good quantity of liquid food. Half a cup of liquid food would allow the exercises to be started in half an hour. At least four hours and a half must elapse between a heavy meal.

15. There is no harm if food is taken in a moderate quantity in something like half an hour after the Yogic exercises.

Place

16. Any well ventilated place may be used for Yogic exercises. The only care to be taken is not to allow the body to be exposed to a strong draught.

Seat

17. For a spiritual culturist the traditional arrangement of seating is excellent. A carpet of Kusa grass * with a well- tanned deer-hide spread on it, the hide in its turn being covered with a daily washed piece of thick khaddar, makes a very comfortable seat. A physical culturist may use a carpet large enough to accommodate the length and breadth of the individual practising Yogic exercise. From the hygienic point of view it is desirable that this carpet also is covered with a daily washed piece of khaddar.

---

* In the absence of Kusa grass carpet, any other grass carpet will serve the purpose. Those that may have a conscientious objection of the use of a hide, should make use of a thick woollen cloth folded over several times.

Time and Sequence

18. Uḍḍiyāna, Nauli, Kapālabhāti or Bhastrikā and Ujjāyi should be practised in the morning, in the sequence in which they have been taken up here.

19. Uḍḍiyāna and Nauli may be practised by the constipated people even before they get the call of nature.

20. Taking a few ounces, say ten to twenty, of tepid water, with a little rock-salt added to it (1 grain per ounce), may be taken before practising Nauli. This will induce a rapid bowel movement.

21. Kapālabhāti or Bhastrikā and Ujjāyī, should follow not only evacuation, but, as far as possible, a full bath. They are best practised in Padmāsana or Siddhāsana although for Kapālbhāti and Bhastrikā, padmāsana is preferable.

22. Āsanas are better gone through in the evening because muscles are more elastic then, than in the morning.

23. Yoga Mudrā so also Ujjāyi and Kapāabhāti or Bhastrikā may be practised also in the evening.

24. Yoga-Mudrā should be taken up with Āsanas and be practised before Śavāsana.

25. Whether in the morning or in the evening, the Yogic exercises should be practised in the following order. First take Āsanas with Yoga-Mudrā, then the Bandha and the Kriyās, and lastly the Prāṇāyāmas. Kapālabhāti should be considered as a part of Prāṇāyāma.

26. In practising Āsanas students will do well to preserve the sequence of the various poses that has been followed in enlisting them here. In getting oneself trained, however, one need not follow this sequence rigorously. One may pick up the different Āsanas in any order he likes, the easiest being taken up first and the more difficult being taken up later on.

27. The omission of a particular practice does not disqualify a student to go through the remaining part of the scheme with advantage.

Combination with Other Exercises

28. There is no harm in undergoing the Yogic exercises and strenuous muscular exercises side by side.

29. But the two should never be practised immediately before one another. At least a period of twenty minutes should be allowed to go by.

30. Those that want to finish their exercises with a balance introduced into their system, should take the Yogic exercises last. But those that want to have spirt of exhalation at the end, should finish with the muscular exercises.

31. Walk when taken as exercise must be brisk, and for consideration of sequence should be treated a muscular exercise. A stroll stands on a different level, and may precede or follow the Yogic practices.

Yogic Exercises and Bath

32. A whole bath should precede the Yogic exercises. Because the same promotes blood circulation uniformly throughout

the body, and the diversion of a richer blood current to a articular part by means of a Yogic exercise becomes easier.

33. But a local bath intended for a particular part of the body for promoting blood circulation therein, should neither precede nor follow the general Yogic exercises immediately, although local baths and particular Yogic exercises may be combined with the advice of an expert.

Food, Drink, Smoke etc.

34. Every man should try to find which food suits him the best irrespective of the dictates of his palate.

35. Even people who maintain more than average health, should restrict themselves to such varieties of food as they find agreeable. Every meal should be of a moderate quantity which must be well masticated, so that it may become freely mixed with the saliva and its digestion may become easier.

36. People with weak digestion should take to low protein diet. They should satisfy themselves with two meals per day and preferably even with one, the place of the other meal being taken by light refreshment.

37. Those who suffer from dyspepsia and constipation or have some uric acid trouble, will do well to eliminate all sorts of pulse. They should also avoid potatoes, brinjals and onions.

38. Water taken half an hour after the meal suits almost every constitution. Those that have their digestive capacity unimpaired may take water along with their food..

39. All alcoholic drinks are to be cautiously avoided. Stimulants

such as tea and coffee are never to be taken in excess and may preferably be eliminated altogether. For a man that cares for his health, there cannot be a more luxurious drink than plain water.

40. Heavy smoking of whatever sort invariably shatters the nerves, if carried on for many years. Weak nerves, persistent cough, sore throat, etc., always harass a heavy smoker; and may often beset the path even of a light smoker.

41. All unnatural and illegitimate sexual acts are sinful. Excess committed even in natural and legitimate sexual acts do not stand on a different footing.

42. No sexual intercourse is healthy unless it is undertaken as a matter of absolute physiological necessity.

Exercises for Boys and Girls

45. Boys and girls will do well, first to start with the SHORT COURSE in every case and to take up the FULL COURSE late on.

46. Boys and girls under 12 would be well advised to restrict themselves to Bhujaṅgāsana, Ardha-Śalabhāsana, Dhanurāsana, Paścimatāna, Halāsana and Yoga-Mudrā only. After 12 the remaining exercises of the FULL COURSE may be taken up.

N.B.- This FULL COURSE and the hints given there on are intended for an average man of health. People falling below the average may try the SHORT COURSE, or better seek expert advice, for being prescribed suitable exercises.

APPENDIX-II

A SHORT COURSE IN YOGIC PHYSICAL CULTURE

1.	Bhujaṅgāsana	...	3 to 7 turns each; the pose being maintained for 2 to 5 secs., one turn being added to each, every fortnight.
2.	Ardha-Śalabhāsana		
3.	Dhanurāsana		
4.	Halāsana	...	First only Ardha-Halāsana to be tried for 2 secs. in each of its stages. Then the full pose may be taken through its four different stages, each stage being maintained for 2 secs. only. 3 to 5 turns adding one turn every fortnight.
5.	Paśchimatāna	...	To be maintained for 5 secs. 3 to 7 turns, adding one turn every fortnight.
6.	Ardha-Matsyendrāsana	...	To be maintained for 5 secs. 3 to 7 turns, adding one turn every fortnight.
7.	Yoga-Mudrā or Uḍḍiyāna	...	To be maintained for 10 secs. 3 to 5 turns, adding one turn per week.
8.	Viparīta Karaṇī	...	First Ardha to be practised with 2 secs., pause at every stage. Afterwards the full pose to be taken with 10 secs., pause. 2 to 5 turns, adding one turn every fortnight.
9.	Ujjāyī	...	7 to 21 rounds, adding 3 rounds per week.

HINTS REGARDING THE SHORT COURSE

1. THE SHORT COURSE is framed for those people who cannot, for want of time, strength or wish, follow the FULL COURSE.
2. All the hints given to Yogic Physical Culturists concerning the FULL COURSE should be applicable to this SHORT COURSE as well as to the EASY COURSE that follows.
3. Exercises tabulated in the SHORT COURSE may be started at the age of 9. Ujjāyī and Uḍḍiyāna should not be begun, however, before 12 or even 13.
4. The SHORT COURSE is available to females as well as to males.
5. Those that can tolerate Yogic exercise in the morning, may, if they so choose, undergo the SHORT COURSE both morning and evening. Others should practise Ujjāyi and Uḍḍiyāna in the morning and the rest of the exercises in the evening. Ujjāyi is to be practised in the evening also.
6. This SHORT COURSE may be made shorter not by omitting any of the practices tabled here, but by undergoing all the exercises on a smaller scale.
7. Although the practice of the SHORT COURSE or of the EASY COURSE tabulated hereafter is comparatively innocent, people suffering from any serious disorder should not undertake exercises on their own responsibility.
8. The EASY COURSE that follows is intended for those who are much run down in health and are suffering from general debility, but have no other specific complaint.

APPENDIX-III

AN EASY COURSE IN YOGIC PHYSICAL CULTURE

1. Ujjāyi	...	7 to 14 rounds, adding 2 rounds per week.
2. Bhujaṅgāsana 3. Ardha-Śalabhāsana	....	2 to 5 turns each. The pose to be maintained for 2 to 5 secs. one turn being added to each every fortnight.
4. Ardha-Halāsana	...	Begin with one leg only. To be practised with both the legs after a fortnight. Rest for 2 secs. at angles of 15^0, 30^0, 60^0, & 90^0; 3 to 6 turns, adding one turn every fortnight.
5. Vakrāsana	...	To be maintained for 5 secs. on each side. 3 to 6 turns, adding one turn every fortnight.
6. Cakrāsana (side bending)	...	To be maintained for 2 secs. on each side. 2 to 5 turns, adding one turn every fortnight.
7. Paścimatāna	...	To be maintained for 3 secs. 2 to 5 turns, adding one turn every fortnight.
8. Yoga-Mudrā or its variation	...	To be maintained for 5 secs. 3 to 5 turns, adding one turn every week.

GLOSSARY

(N.B. - References to pages refer to the body of this handbook. Greek or Latin origin of words is given in the glossary. Sanskrit origin being given in the body of the handbook is omitted from here.)

(Grk. = Greek; Lat. = Latin; Skr. = Sanskrit).

Abdomen, adj. abdominal, the belly.

Abdominal Aorta, part of the aorta situated in the abdomen. see aorta.

Abdominal breathing, that type of respiration in which the abdominal movement is prominent. (*Vide* p. 18).

Ābhyantara (Skr.), internal; coming after inhalation.

Absorption (Lat. *absorbere,* to suck up), the process by which the circulatory system picks up nutritive elements from the digestive system.

Accomplished Pose, Siddhāsana. (*Vide* p. 31).

Adam's Apple, popular name of the thyroid cartilage.

Afferent, see nerves.

Air-Cells, the extremely small circular bags in the substance of the lungs into which the inhaled air passes and across which it is diffused into the blood current.

Alveolus, pl. alveoli, adj. alveolar, a small cavity; an air-cell of the lung.

Anal Contraction, Mula-Bandha. (*Vide* p. 29).

Anal Sphincters, the two sphincters situated an inch apart at the two ends of the anal canal which forms the last part of the colon. The lower and sexual sphincter constitutes the anus.

Anatomy (Grk. ana, apart, and temno, I cut), adj. anatomical, the science which deals with the structure of organized bodies.

Anterior, more to the front.

Anus (Lat. the sitting part), adj. anal, the terminal of the rectum.

Aorta (Gr. aeiro I take up or carry), the great trunk of the arterial system issuing from the left side of the heart.

Apex of the Nose, the free end of the nose.

Apnoea or Apnea (Grk. a, not an pneo, I breathe), Transient cessation of respiration. (*Vide* p. 37).

Arterialization, the process of turning the venous into arterial blood.

Artery, ad. arterial, one of the tubes through which the heart propels the blood to the different parts of the body.

Āsana (Skr.), a Yogic pose.

Atmospheric Pressure, pressure equal to that of a column of mercury about thirty inches of 760 mm. in height.

Auditory (Lat. audio, I hear), of the organ or sense of hearing.

Auditory Tubes, see Eustachain tube.

Auspicious pose, Svastikāsana. (*Vide* p. 32)

Āyama (Skr.), a control. (*Vide* p. 35).

Bāhya (skr.), external; coming after exhalation.

Bandha (Skr.), a fixed arrangement of contracted muscles. (*Vide* p. 24).

Basti (Skr.), the bellows.

Bhagavān (Skr.), glorious. The word is also used in a technical sense which is not intended in this text.

Bhastrā (Skr.), the bellows.

Bhastrikā (Skr), a variety of Prāṇāyāma characterized by incessant explorations followed by Kumbhaka. See Chapter VI.

Bhrāmari (Skr.), one of the eight varieties of Prāṇāyāma wherein a student of Yoga imitates the humming of bees during inhalations and exhalations.

Bhrūmadhya-Dṛiṣṭi (Skr), the Frontal Gaze. This requires fixing one's eyes between the eyebrows. (*Vide* p. 23).

Blood-Vessel, a flexible tube such as an artery or a vein that conveys blood.

Brahmānanda, a comentator of *Haṭha Pradīpikā.*

Brain, the mass of nervous substance in the skull responsible for the expression of the various faculties of the mind.

Breast Bone, the this flat vertical bone in the chest connecting the ribs in the front.

Bridge of the Nose, the structures formed by the two nasal bones.

Bronchus (Grk. bronchos), pl. bronchi, adj. bronchial, one of the two branches into which the windpipe bifurcates in the chest.

Canine tooth, the sixth tooth in the upper and lower jaws which is pointed and resembles a corresponding tooth in dog.

Capillary (Lat. capillus, a hair), a minute blood-vessel connecting the smallest ramifications of the arteries with those of the veins.

Carbon-dioxide, carbonic acid gas; CO_2.

Cardiac (Grk. *kardia,* the heart), of the heart.

Cardiac sphincter, the circular muscle fibres around the cardiac end of the oesophagus.

Carotid arteries, the two principal large arteries one on each side of the neck.

Carotid sinus, a slight dilatation of the common carotid artery.

Cartilage (Lat. cartilago), adj. cartilaginous, gristle; a firm but elastic anatomical structure such as that forming the external ear or nose.

Cell, an ultimate element of organic structures.

Central (STIMULUS), given to the internal surface.

Central Canal, small canal that extends throughout the centre of the spinal cord.

Central Nervous System, see nervous system.

Cervical Vertebrae, see vertebra.

Cakra (Skr.). a nerve-centre of spiritual significance.

Candra-Nāḍī (Skr.), Iḍā; the left nostril. (*Vide* p. 47).

Chin-Lock, Jālandhara-Bandha. (*Vide* p. 27).

Cilia, sin. cilium, minute hair-like vibrating organs on the surface of the epithelium, forming there a sort of brush.

Ciliated Epithelium, see cila and epithelium.

Circulatory System, the system consisting of organs responsible for the circulation of the blood; they are the heart, the arteries, the veins and the capillaries.

Clavicle, the collar-bone.

Coccygeal, n. coccyx, of the coccyx. See vertebra.

Complemental air, the difference in quantity of air inhaled in the normal and the deepest inspiration.

Congestion, an abnormal accumulation of the blood in a part of the body.

Constipation, inability of the colon throw out of its foecal contents.

Coastal breathing (Lat. costa, a rib), that type of respiration in which the movement of the ribs is prominent. (*Vide* p. 18).

Cranial Nerves, see nerves.

Cranium (Grk. kranion, the skull), adj. cranial, the skull; bones enclosing the brain.

Cricoid Cartilage (Grk. krikos, a ring, and eidos, likeness), a prominent cartilage forming the larynx. (*Vide* p. 9).

Dhārṇā (Skr.), concentrating the mind upon one point.

Dhauti (Skr.), the Yogic method of cleansing and massaging the stomach.

Dhyāna (skr.), continuous flow of the same ideation.

Diaphragm (Grk. diaphragma, a partition), adj. diaphragmatic, the big muscle that forms the flow of the thorax separating it from the abdomen.

Diaphragmatic Breathing, the same as the abdominal breathing.

Diffusion of Gases, intermingling of gases held in different enclosures communicating with one another either directly or across a thin partition.

Digestive System, this consists of the organs of digestion, such as the stomach, the small intestine, the colon, etc.

Dṛṣṭi (Skr.), gaze

Dyspepsia (Grk. dys, ill, and pepso, I digest), adj. dyspetic, indisgetion.

Efferent, see nerves.

Elastic Recoil, forceful shrinkage in size of an elastic substance like a piece of India-rubber or the lungs after it is stretched.

Endocrine Glands (Grk. endon, within, and krino, I separate out), glands which produce an internal secretions.

Endocrinology, the study of the internal secretions.

Epiglottis (Grk, epi, upon, and *glottis*, the upper opening of the wind pipe), the erect cartilage situated at the root of the tongue. It is depressed during the action of swallowing to cover the glottis and thus to prevent food going a wrong way. (*Vide* p. 8).

Epithelium (Grk. epi, upon, and *thele*, a *nipple*), a delicate tissue forming the outer layer of the mucous membrane.

Ethmoid (Grk. *ethmos*, a sieve, and *eidos,* likeness), the big bone which forms a part of the nasal roof. (*Vide* p. 4).

Eustachain Orifices, the pharyngeal openings of the auditory tubes.

Eustachian Tubes, canals connecting the pharynx with the cavities of the ears; the auditory tubes. The pharyngeal openings of these tubes are called the Eustachian orifices. (*Vide* p.7).

Flexors, muscles that bend the different parts of the body, such as the legs, the thighs, etc.

Foot-Lock, a lock prepared by a particular arrangement of the legs. (*Vide* p.30).

Frontal Gaze, Bhrūmadhya-Dṛiṣṭi. (*Vide* p. 23).

Gangliated Cords, nervous chains furnished with ganglia.

Ganglion (Grk.), pl. ganglia, a well-defined collection of nerve cells and fibres forming a subordinate nerve-centre.

Gastric (Grk. gaster, the stomach), related to the stomach.

Gheraṇḍa-Saṃhitā (Skr.), a text book of Haṭha-Yoga.

Gland (lat. *glans*, an acorn), an organ composed of cells secreting constituents of the blood.

Glottis (Grk.), an opening between the vocal cords situated in the windpipe. (*Vide* p. 10).

Gout, disease with inflammation of smaller joints.

Groin, the depression between the belly and the thigh.

Guptāsana (Skr.), the same as Samāsana. (*Vide* p. 34).

Hard Palate, the hard part of the roof of the mouth.

Haṭha (Skr.), Haṭha-Yoga; that system of Yoga which starts with the purification of the body as the first step towards spiritual perfection.

Haṭha Pradīpikā (Skr.), the most authoritative text of Haṭha - Yoga.

Heart, the muscular pump situated in the chest that keeps up the blood circulating in the body.

Hydrocele (Grk. *hydor*, water, and *kele*, a tumour), collection of watery fluid around or near the testicle.

Iḍā (Skr.), Candra-Nāḍī; the left nostril. (*Vide* p. 47).

Iliac Bones, the two side bones in the lower portion of the abdomen.

Impulse (NERVE), a sort of disturbance or push travelling across the nerves.

Incisors, the 7th and 8th teeth in the jaws that are useful in cutting.

Intercostal (Lat. inter, between and *costa,* a rib), situated between the ribs.

Internalize, turn inward.

Interoceptic, belonging to interaceptors.

Interceptor, any one of the end organs situated in the viscera which receive stimuli from visceral activities, such as digestion, excretion, circulation.

Intra-abdominal, inside the cavity of the abdomen.

Intra-pulmonic, inside the cavity of the lungs.

Intra-thoracic, inside the cavity of the chest.

Jālandhara-Bandha (Skr.), the Chin-Lock, requiring the chin to be closely pressed against the chest.

Jaw bone, one of the two bones that from the skeleton of the mouth.

Jñāna-Mudrā (Skr.), the Symbol of Knowledge. (*Vide* p. 50).

Jugular Notch (Lat. jugulur, the throat), the depression below the throat and between the two collar bones.

Kapālabhāti (Skr.), one of the Ṣaṭ Kriyās consisting of a breathing exercise for the purification of the body. It is characterized by incessant expirations. see Chapter V.

Kevala (Skr.), pure; without inhalation or exhalation. (*Vide* p. 37).

Kidneys, the two abdominal organs which are mainly concerned in the excretion of urine.

Kriyā (Skr.), any Yogic exercise, especially any of the six cleansing processes. Also see Ṣaṭ Kriyās.

Kumbhaka (Skr.), see Prāṇāyāma.

Kuṇḍdalinī (Skr.), the spiritual energy ordinarily locked up in an abdominal nal centre. (*Vide* p. 73).

Kuśa, (skr.) a kind of sacred grass.

Laryngeal Pharynx, the lowermost portion of the pharynx situated in the throat just above the larynx. (*Vide* larynx and pharynx).

Larynx (Lat. laryngx), adj. laryngeal, the cavity forming the voice-box situated in the throat below the pharynx.

Lateral, situated on the side. (*Vide* 9. 8)

Lingual, of the tongue.

Liver, a large glandular organ that manufactures bile and purifies the venous blood.

Lotus Pose, Padmāsana. (*Vide* p. 30).

Lower Extremities, legs.

Lung Capacity, this is indicated by the vital capacity plus 1600 ml. of air. (*Vide* p. 12).

Lungs, the two breathing organs situated in the chest. (*Vide* p. 12).

Massage, rubbing, kneading or otherwise manipulating the muscles and joints for stimulating their action.

Mātrā (Skr.), a time-unit. (*Vide* p 40).

Mediastinal Cavity (Lat. *medius*, middle), the cavity that separates the two lungs. (*Vide* p. 15).

Membrane, adj. membranous, pliable sheet-like lining in the human body.

Metabolism (Grk. *metabole*, change), the process of assimilation of food and its conversion into energy.

Molars, grinding teeth, the first three teeth in the upper and lower jaws.

Motor Nerves, nerves responsible for the muscular activity. Also see nerves.

Mucous Membrane, a membrane secreting a slimmy substance called mucus, such as covers our lips.

Mudrā (Skr.), a symbol.

Mūla-Bandha (Skr.) the Anal Contraction which requires vigorous contraction of the sphincters of the anus. (*Vide* p. 29).

Murcchā or Murcchanā (Skr.), one of the eight varieties of Prāṇāyāma which is peculiarly capable of rendering the mind passive. (*Vide* pp. 65 and 101).

Muscle, any of the contractile fibrous bundles that chiefly constitute flesh. Muscles are of two kinds, the striped or striated and the smooth or unstriated. The striped muscles are voluntary and the smooth are involuntary. Involuntary muscles are not subject to the will.

Nāḍī (Skr.), a nerve; a nostril.

Nāḍīśuddhi (Skr.), physiological balance necessary for spiritual development. (*Vide* p. 75).

Nāsāgra Dṛṣṭi (Skr.), the Nasal Gaze. This requires fixing one's eyes upon one's tip of the nose. (*Vide* p. 23).

Nasal Bones, the two bones of the nose standing between the eyes and below the forehead. (*Vide* p. 3).

Nasal Gaze, Nāsāgra Dṛṣṭi. (*Vide* p. 23).

Nasal Pharynx, that portion of the pharynx which is situated above the soft palate. (*Vide* larynx and pharynx).

Nauli or Naulika, one of the Ṣaṭ Kriyās, being an abdominal exercise consisting of the rolling manipulations of the isolated recti.

Nerve Centure, a group of nerve-cells functioning together.

Nerves, fine thread-like or wire-like structures connecting the brain and the spinal cord with the different parts of the body. Message running to and from across these wires are responsible for different sensations experienced by man and the various movements he makes. The nerves responsible for the muscular activity are called the motor of efferent nerves, whereas those that convey sensations from the ends to the different centres are called the sensory or afferent nerves. System consisting of these wire-like structures together with the brain and the spinal cord, manages all the voluntary and involuntary functions of the human body.

Nervous System, see nerves. All the nerves put together, form the nervous system. It consists of two divisions, the central or cerebro-spinal system and the automatic system. The latter is subdivided into two parts, the para-sympathetic and the sympathetic. The central nervous system mainly consists of the brain, twelve pairs of the cranial nerves, the spinal cord and thirty one pairs of the spinal nerves. The sympathetic is chiefly represented by two chains of ganglia placed one on each side of spinal column, the para-sympathetic is found near the brain and the sacrum.

Neti (Skr.), one of the Ṣaṭ Kriyās for cleansing the nasal passage by means of a wick inserted through the nose and extracted through the mouth or by means of water passed through the nose.

Nostrils, the two openings in the nose.

OEsophagus, (Grk. oiso, I bear, and *phagein*, to eat), adj. oesophageal, the canal extending from the throat to the stomach, some nine to ten inches in length, through which food and drink pass; the gullet.

Olfactory Bulb, the bulbous end of the olfactory nerve.

Olfactory nerves (Lat. *oleo,* I smell, and *facio*, I make), nerves responsible for the sense of smell.

Olfactory Region, the upper third of the nasal cavities which contains the sense of smell. (*Vide* p. 5).

Optic Nerves (Grk. *ops*, the eye), nerves responsible for the sense of sight.

Oral Pharynx, that portion of the pharynx which is situated behind the mouth and the tongue. (*Vide* larynx and pharynx).

Padmāsāna, (Skr.), the Lotus Pose. (*Vide* p. 30).

Pancreas (Grk. pan all, and kreas flesh), a gland that is situated near the stomach and that provides a digestive secretion to the system.

Para-Sympathetic, see nervous system.

Parietal (Lat. *paries*, a wall), of the wall of the body or of any of its cavities. Thus the parietal layer of the pleurae is the layer which lines the inner surface of the thoracic cavities. (*Vide* p. 14).

Patañjali, the author of Yoga Sūtras. The first systematic exponent of Yoga philosophy.

Pelvis (Lat. a basin), adj. pelvic, the lowermost part of the abdominal cavity between the hip-bones.

Perineum (Grk. *peri,* about, and *naio*, to be situated), the portion between the genitals and the anus.

Peripheral (STIMULUS), given to the external surface.

Pharynx (Lat. *pharyngx*), adj. pharyngeal, cavity with enclosing muscles and mucous membrane situated behind the nose, mouth and larynx. This cavity has openings which individually communicate with each of these organs.

Physiology (Grk. *physis,* nature, and *logos,* a discourse), adj. physiological, science of the normal functions of living organisms.

Piṅgalā (Skr.), Sūrya-Nāḍī; the right nostril. (*Vide* p. 46).

Pituitary, a ductless gland situated in the upper region of the central nervous system.

Plavini (Skr.), one of the eight varieties of Prāṇāyāma which enables one to float on water very comfortably.

Pleura (Grk. *pleuron,* a rib), pl. pleurae, one of the two serous membranes lining the thorax and enveloping the lungs.

Pleural Cavity, the space between the two layers of the pleurae.

Pleurisy, inflammation of the pleura. (*Vide* p. 14).

Plexus (Lat. a network), a tangle of nerves and blood-vessels.

Pneumogastric Nerve, the vagus nerve. It is the most extensive of the cranial nerves distributed to the lungs, the heart, the stomach, etc., and is notable responsible for the movements of the respiratory muscles.

Posterior, adv. posterior, more to the back side.

Pracchardana (Skr.), Recaka. (*Vide* p. 39).

Prāṇa (Skr.), breath. (*Vide* p. 35).

Prāṇāyāma (Skr.), adj. Prāṇāyāmic, the fourth item of Yogic curriculum. Yogic breath control. Kumbhaka. (*Vide* p. 37). According to Svātmārāma Sūri there are eight varieties of Prāṇāyāma. They are: Sūryabhedana, Ujjāyī, Sītkārī, Śītalī, Bhastrikā, Bhrāmarī, Mūrccha and Plāvinī.

Praśvāsa (Skr.), the air flowing out of the lungs. (*Vide* p. 36).

Pratyāhāra (Skr.), introversion of the mind.

Premolar, the 4th and 5th teeth in the upper and lower jaws.

Presso-Receptor, a nerve ending as in the carotid sinus, which is stimulated by changes in the blood-pressure.

Psychology (Grk. *psyche* the mind, and *logos,* a discourse), that branch of science which treats of the mind and mental operations.

Pubic Bone (Lat. *pubis,* puberty), the bone just above the genitals.

Pulmonary, Pulmonic (Lat. *pulmo*, a lung), of the lungs.

Pūraka (Skr.), inhalation. (*Vide* p. 38).

Rāja-Yoga (Skr.), samādhi. The eighth item of Yogic curriculum.

Recaka (Skr.), exhalation. (*Vide* p. 38).

Rectum (Lat. *rectus,* straight), the last part of the bowel.

Reserve Air, the same as supplement air.

Residual Air, that quantity of air which is left in the lungs even after the deepest possible expiration. (*Vide* p. 19).

Respiration (Lat. *respiration*), breathing.

Respiratory Capacity, the same as vital capacity.

Respiratory Centre, a nerve centre from which respiratory activities are governed.

Respiratory Region, the lower two-thirds of the nasal cavities, (*Vide* p. 5).

Respiratory System, this consists of the organs of respiration, such as the lungs, the trachea etc. (*Vide* p.1).

Root of the Nose, the upper end of the nose.

Sacral, n. sacrum, belonging to the bone sacrum. See vertebra.

Sādhaka (Skr.), an aspirant trying to evolve himself spiritually.

Samādhi (Skr.), the eighth stage in Yogic evolution wherein the individual either stands face to face with the Infinite or becomes entirely merged into it.

Samāsana (Skr.), the Symmetrical Pose. (*Vide* p. 34).

Scroll-like, circularly curved upon themselves.

Secretion, juice manufactured by a gland to fulfil some useful physiological function. When this secretion is thrown directly into the blood current it is called internal; but when it is conducted through tubes called ducts the secretion is called external.

Sensory Nerves, nerves that convey sensations from ends to the centres. Also see nerves.

Septum, partition such as that between the two nostrils.

Serous Membrane, a smooth glistening membrane that secretes lubricating fluid.

Ṣaṭ Kriyās (Skr.), the six cleansing processes prescribed in Haṭha-Yoga for the purification of the body. They are: Dhauti, Basti, Neti, Trātaka, Nauli and Kapābhāti. (*Vide* p. 61).

Siddhāsana (Skr.), the Accomplished Pose. (*Vide* p. 31).

Sinus Nerve, nerve connected with the carotid sinus.

Śītalī (Skr.), one of the eight varieties of Prāṇyāma characterized by oral inhalations wherein the tongue is projected outside the mouth in a beaklike arrangement. Śītalī has a cooling effects upon the whole system.

Sītkārī (Skr.), one of the eight varieties of Prāṇāyāma characterized by a wheezing sound, sound that is produced by a peculiar arrangement of the teeth and the tongue during inspirations.

Śiva-Saṃhitā (Skr.), a text-book of Haṭha-Yoga.

Soft Palate, the soft part of the roof of the mouth.

Sphincter, (Grk. *sphingo*, I bind), muscular structure which surrounds a tube or an opening and closes the same by its contraction.

Spinal Column, Spine, back-bone. See vertebra.

Spinal Cord, the tail of the brain which descends into the vertebral column. Also see nervous system.

Spinal Nerves, see nervous system.

Srīkṛṣna, the eighth incarnation of the Lord.

Stemum (Lat.), the breastbone.

Stimulus, pl. stimuli, thing evoking functional reaction.

Stomach, principal organ of digestion, situated in the abdomen in continuation of the gullet.

Supplemental Air, the difference in quantity of air expelled in the normal and the deepest expiration. (*Vide* p. 19).

Sūryabhedana (Skr.), one of the eight varieties of Prāṇāyāma characterized by invariable inhalations through Surya, that is, the right nostril and exhalations through the opposite one with a pause in between the two.

Sūrya-Nāḍī (Skr.), Piṅgalā or the right nostril. (*Vide* p. 47).

Suṣumnā (Skr.), the spinal cord.

Sūtra (Skr.), an aphorism.

Śvāsa (Skr.), the air flowing into the lungs. (*Vide* p. 36).

Svasthkāsana (Skr.), the Auspicious Pose (*Vide* p. 32).

Svātmārāma Sūri, the author of Haṭha Pradīpikā the most authoritative textbook of Haṭha-Yoga.

Symmetrical Pose, Samāsana. (*Vide* p. 34).

Sympathetic, see nervous system.

System, a combination of parts into a whole, as the digestive system, nervous system etc.,

Therapeutics, Therapy (Grk *therapeuo,* I treat or cure), adj. therapeutical, science of healing. *Thorax* (Grk.), adj. thoracic, the chest.

Thyroid, a ductless gland situated in the neck.

Thyroid Cartilage, a prominent cartilage forming the larynx (*Vide* p. 9)

Tidal Air, the volume of air that constantly and uniformly flows out and flows in normal respiration. (*Vide* p. 19).

Tissue, a distinct structure formed of similar cells and cell products.

Toxins (Grk. toxikon, poison), adj. toxic, posions.

Trachea (Lat.), the principal air passage forming the windpipe. Some four inches in length, it starts in the throat and descends into the chest. (*Vide* p. 10).

Trātaka, one of the Ṣaṭ Kriyās being an exercise in gazing.

Trunk, human body without head and limbs.

Uḍḍiyāna-Bandha (Skr.), the raising of the diaphragm. (*Vide* p. 24).

Ujjāyī (Skr.), a variety of Prāṇāyāma characterized by a smooth frictional sound through the throat, due to partial closure of the glottis in breath ing. See Chapter IV.

Uvula, the conical appendix hanging from the free edge of the palate.

Vagus Nerve (Lat, *vagus*, wandering), the same as the pneumogatric nerve, so called because of its wide distribution.

Vascular Lat. *vasculum*, a vessel), n. vascularity, richly supplied with vessels such as blood-vessels.

Vein, adj. venous, one of the tubes which carry the blood from the different parts of the body to the heart.

Ventricles (Lat. *ventrticulus*, diminutive of venter, the belly), cavities in the interior of the brain or heart.

Vertebra (Lat. a joint), pl. vertabrae, adj. vertebral, each of the thirty-three pieces which form the backbone. The topmost seven are called the cervical, the next twelve the dorsal, the next five lumbar, the next five the sacral and the last four the coccygeal.

Vertebral Column, the spine.

Vestibule of the Nose, the lowest chamber of the internal nose. (*Vide* p. 2).

Vidhārana (Skr.), Kumbhaka. (*Vide* p. 38).

Viscera, adj, visceral, the interior organs in the great cavities of the body, especially in the abdomen.

Visceral Layer, the inner layer of the pleura which is adherent to the lungs.

Vital Capacity, the capacity indicated by the largest quantity of air, a man can inhale after the deepest possible expiration (*Vide* p. 19).

Vital Index, this represents lung capacity divided by body weight.

Vocal Cords, the laryngeal folds of the mucous membrane which are responsible for the production of voice. (*Vide* p. 10).

Vyāsa, the first known commentator of Patañjali's Yoga-Sūtras.

Wind-pipe, the principal air passage some four inches in length. It starts in the throat and descends into the chest.

X-rays, kind of rays penetrating many substances impervious to ordinary light and thus extending the field of human vision.

Yoga (Skr.), adj. Yogic, a system of exercises, physical or mental, which may begin with the purification of the body and which culminate in a stage wherein the individual soul becomes merged into the Infinite.

Yoga-Śāstra (Skr.), logically systematized art and science of Yoga.

Yogic physical Culture, a systematic training of physiological functions through the exercises prescribed in Yoga.

Yogic Therapeutics, Yogic Therapy, the science and art of healing by means of Yogic exercises.

KAIVALYADHAMA
MUMBAI

KAIVALYADHAMA

Where Yoga tradition and Science meet

KAIVALYADHAMA

Where Yoga tradition and Science meet